Hogs In The Bottom

Hogs In The Bottom
Family Folklore In Arkansas
By Deirdre LaPin
With Louis Guida and Lois Pattillo

August House

Original photographs of Amalite Fratesi and Ivan Johnson by Louis Guida. Other original photographs by Deirdre La Pin.

Folklore/Ethnic Studies/Southern Studies

Copyright 1982 by Deirdre LaPin.
Published 1982 by August House, Inc.,
1010 West Third Street, Little Rock, AR 72201
All rights reserved. No part of this book
may be reproduced in any form or manner without
the prior written consent of the publisher.

First Printing: July, 1982

ISBN 0-935304-36-3 Hardback
ISBN 0-935304-39-8 Paperback

Library of Congress Catalog Card Number: 82-70164
LaPin, Deirdre
Hogs in the Bottom
Little Rock: August House
July, 1982

This publication was made possible, in part, by a grant from the Arkansas Endowment for the Humanities, Dr. Anthony Dubé, Executive Director, Jane Browning, Assistant Director.

For our families

Deirdre LaPin, director of the Family Folklore in Central Arkansas Project, teaches folklore in the Department of English at the University of Arkansas at Little Rock. Her doctorate at the University of Wisconsin drew upon five years of field research on narrative traditions among the Yoruba people of SW Nigeria. Since joining the UALR faculty, she has encouraged the documentation of Arkansas culture through the University's Regional Studies Program, through her courses on Family Folklore, and by consulting on a number of Arkansas cultural heritage projects. Her publications include over a dozen articles and essays, two films, and two books.

Louis Guida has directed project work on Arkansas' immigrant Italian farmers for a Rockefeller Foundation Humanities survey and for the Southeast Arkansas Arts and Science Center in Pine Bluff. In 1976 he served as field collector and director of the Blues Project at the University of Arkansas at Pine Bluff. His articles have appeared in numerous publications, including *Center for Southern Folklore Magazine, Living Blues*, and *American Preservation*. His photographs are included in the permanent collections of museums and cultural centers throughout the United States.

Lois Pattillo — teacher, author, publisher, and poet — has an M.S. degree from the University of Arkansas and has done advanced study at Florida State University. She has received many awards, including an honorary Doctorate of Humane Letters from Shorter College for outstanding humanitarian service. She is research associate on the Family Folklore project and the author of the book *Little Rock Roots*, a collection of biographies of Black Arkansans.

Table of Contents

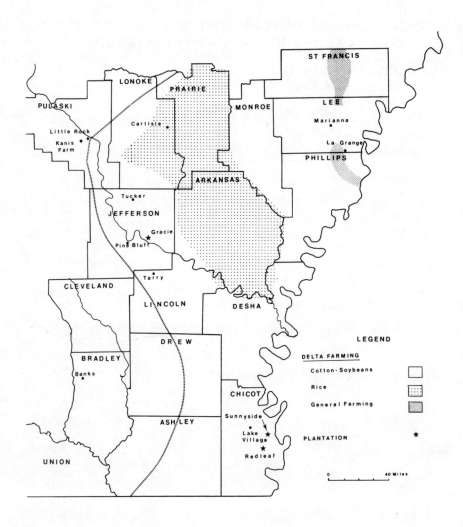

Preface

Since the early seventies, Americans have witnessed a growing interest in the nation's family "roots." Encouraging this trend is a new corresponding branch of folklore studies called "family folklore." While it can be granted that many varieties of folklore depend on the family and its members for transmission, family folklore alone attempts to examine the cultural heritage that bears on the family itself.

The families whose lives and traditions fill the pages of this book were subjects in the project, "Family Folklore in Central Arkansas," funded by the Arkansas Endowment for the Humanities. The purpose of the project was grounded in the following idea: the family, as the most important force in defining the identity of every person, achieves this end by building a repository of creative expressions that bear witness to the common history of every family member. These creative expressions may take the form of oral traditions, customs and celebrations, visual records and artifacts. Examples of each category vary with regional or ethnic bias, but they may include sayings, humorous anecdotes, family reunions, holidays, photograph albums, scrapbooks, home movies and an infinite variety of keepsakes. Indeed, there is no greater storehouse of cultural materials bearing on the "person" — and ultimately the community or region as a collection of persons — than the verbal and material expressions of a family past.

To the extent that nearly every adult is a historian, collector, or archivist in his or her family, exposure to the notion and techniques of family folklore is immediately and compellingly relevant. If anthropology seeks to "turn the stranger into a native," folklore aims to "turn the native into a stranger" and equip him to view his everyday habits with objective distance. This humanistic perspective on the family unites the interests and objectives of scholars with the quite natural desire of family members to take stock of their own heritage.

Our families were selected from many whom we learned about through word-of-mouth, knew by personal contact (or through blood ties, as in the case of Lois Pattillo and the Peyton-Hill family), or met after they responded to newspaper articles about our work. While we would maintain that every family is a fitting subject for a family folklore collector, this sample developed from the following criteria: each family has lived in eastern or central Arkansas for at least three generations; together the families represent a cross-section of nationalities and ethnic groups that settled in the region; the families are evenly distributed within the geography of central and southeastern Arkansas; most adult family members have been engaged in work activities traditional to their environment; family members exhibited a reasonable level of mutual awareness and cohesion; all of the families exhibited enthusiasm for the project and an openness with the researchers. In so far as possible, all family members were involved in our interviews, but the strength of our information usually depended on one or two family members who came forward as the spokespeople for the group. Assuming the role of ex-officio researchers, they became valued liaisons between the research team and their subjects; it was they who took charge of collecting folklore materials and keeping the researchers abreast of family events. Four to nine visits were made to each liaison, often with other family members present. Without their generous voluntary assistance, our work would not have been done.

It is generally recognized that folklorists, by lending validity to the past, do far more than document phenomena; their concern also helps to foster the continuation of the folklore process in a way that ensures its preservation in people's lives. We hope that the case studies and collecting guide included here will encourage more families to document their cultural heritage, thereby adding not merely to their knowledge of their kin, but to their understanding of the cultural elements from which this nation was made.

Deirdre LaPin
Little Rock
24 December 1981

Acknowledgements

Our deepest thanks go to the seven families who, with customary Arkansas hospitality, graciously drew us into their homes, their lore, their keepsakes, their photographs, and often their family celebrations. To the family members who shared long hours with us we owe a special debt: Stephanie and Bill Dixon, Willa Stein Odom, Willie Mae Allen, Estelle Johnson, Linda Tolefree, Ivan Johnson, Amalite and Dan Fratesi, Mary Louise Richardson, Shirley Hill, Marguerite Henry, Edwina Atkinson, Eddie J. Callaway Jr., Lucy Harris, Sadie Owens, Everett and Francis Tucker, Jr., and Mrs. Marion Williams.

We are grateful to the Arkansas Endowment for the Humanities for its generous support of the Family Folklore in Central Arkansas Project and for its contribution to the publication of this book. Many thanks also to Jon Le May for his fine photocopying and printing, to Gerald Hanson for his very helpful map, to Steve Zeitlin and Holly Cutting-Baker for bibliographical material, to Janet Nyberg Paraschos and George West for their editing, encouragement, and advice, and to the many students and friends who shared with us their insights and their lore.

Introduction

This book is not about hogs. It is about the families of men and women who have lived with hogs and have created a folklore about them ... and about themselves. In Arkansas the mere utterance of the word "hogs" evokes a welter of images: rugged fierceness, indomitable will, a natural ability to survive, a proud individualism, and an unshakable adherence to tradition. They are traits that originated in an animal, but gradually they have merged with the world of men. The word "hog" is sometimes synonymous with "person."

The heroes and heroines of this book are "hogs" of a gentler breed than the famed razorbacks encountered by the Ozark mountaineers. Legend tells us that the razorbacks were descendants of a herd De Soto brought on shipboard to the coast of Florida in 1539. From there they escaped into the southern woodlands and, according to Otto Rayburn, became "lords of the wilderness. To shoot into such a mass of fury," he reports, "was almost the same as suicide unless the man behind the gun was an expert marksman and had a steady aim."[1] Somewhat later in history, hogs and their keepers came to occupy the bottomlands of the Mississippi River in the southeastern and central parts of the state. These Delta folks, like their Ozark brethren, developed a close identification with their porcine neighbors, but they endowed the animals with one significant additional trait: the mysterious power of natural increase. In the lowlands a farmer who kept "hogs in the bottom" could expect them to feed on plenty of acorns and hickory nuts and then multiply in short order. Therefore, any man who put one or two hogs in the woods had a claim that allowed him to hunt and kill hogs in untold numbers; moreover, he could start again every year without replenishing his supply. To the Delta farmer hogs meant security, comfort, growth, and a high-yielding investment. For this reason when people say: "We've got hogs in the bottom!" or "bottoms", it means that they are entitled to a share of the neighborhood wealth.

The wealth to which we lay claim in this book is a human product having features similar to the natural, high-yielding, home-grown qualities of hogs. Our subject is the lore that evolves from a lifetime of communication between members of families. Many of us are unconscious of the rich heritage of stories, sayings, celebrations, foods, keepsakes, and homesteads that express our common history and identity as family members. As reminders of our origins, these examples of family folklore may be as permanent as the family homeplace or as fleeting as

[1]Otto Rayburn, *Ozark Folks and Folklore*. TS. Eureka Springs, Arkansas, n.d. Available in Special Collections, University of Arkansas Library, Fayetteville, Arkansas.

Thanksgiving dinner, Dad's favorite joke, or Mom's raspberry jam cake. Yet even these last, non-permanent varieties of lore have a remarkable power to survive. Our willingness to pass them along — and eventually hand them down to later generations — is proof of the continuing pleasure they bring to us...and often to our friends. Indeed, families are not isolated entities; their lore undergoes a constant exchange with the tales and customs of their parent communities. The more expert we become in identifying the traditional expressions of our own family, the better we appreciate the cultural heritage of the region from which we come.

In the next several pages of this book we shall discuss the most common forms of family folklore and illustrate them with examples from friends, students and members of our own family. We shall also look at the ways in which these forms are created and re-created in the course of family life. Finally, we shall comment on their kinship with the folklore of nations, regions, and other families.

This introductory section is followed by seven chapters, each devoted to the folklore of a nuclear (parents and children) family living in central or southeastern Arkansas. Here, folklore will be seen as a vital component in the ongoing experience of family life. Early in our conversations with these families we discovered that many of their folklore items had evolved around themes central to their particular identity. For example, the Peyton family in Carlisle, Arkansas, draws on narratives about a Cherokee ancestor to support the family theme of creativity and self-reliance. Additional expressions of the same idea appear in the admonitions of their father Charley Peyton, who told his children before his death, "be creative," "be independent." His wish has been fulfilled in other family traditions: preferred professions (nursing, teaching), avocations (poem- and song-writing and gardening), and craft traditions and skills (quilting, ceramics, dressmaking).

A concluding chapter, "Be Your Family Folklorist," brings our discussion home. Interviewing relatives, transcribing tapes, building a family archives, copying old photographs and researching genealogies are some of the ways in which family folklore can be captured and preserved. Here, we invite you to set your hogs in the bottom with ours; for we believe that their offspring — as ever-multiplying studies of family folklore — will be our crowning achievement.

THE DYNAMICS OF FAMILY FOLKLORE. What is folklore? How does it work? Folklore can be defined in many ways, and one of the handiest, if least academic, definitions I know was passed on to me by the great collector of Ozark folklore, Vance Randolph. "Folklore," he said, "is traditional material you don't learn in school." What Vance meant is that folklore equips a person with an education, but it does so informally and usually as part of a communicative process that begins almost at birth — as soon as we are able to decipher the words and

14

gestures around us — and continues until the end of our lives.

Probing the definition further, we might ask several more questions. From whom is folklore learned? What kind of material constitutes folklore? What is meant by "traditional?" When and where does a folklore education take place? The answers to these questions will lead us directly to the four elements of the folklore "process," that is, the means by which folk items are transmitted or handed down from one person to the next. These elements are: (1) the folk group (2) the forms of folklore (3) the folk performance (4) the folk event. As interlocking parts of a process, these four elements are difficult to separate, but for the purposes of our extended definition, we shall discuss them individually and then show how they fit together.

People become custodians and creators of folklore, not as isolated persons, but by virtue of their membership in a *folk group*. These human clusters develop from a variety of sources: ethnic, occupational, regional, recreational, or — in the case of family groups — biological. Their character as "folk" groups (distinguished from a military "unit," a women's "group," a soccer "team," a country "club") develops from the spontaneous, informal, and continuing contacts between group members. A logging outfit in which the loggers participate in only job-related communications is not a folk group. But if their contacts eventually generate additional modes of communication that express the logger's particular culture and experience, the folklore process has begun. Vocabulary, clothing, customs, and songs contribute to the logger's folklore. It is occasioned by, but is not a part of, his occupation.

Families are among the easiest folk groups to identify. Their basic criterion for membership is a bond of marriage or blood. Modern Americans often regard the word "family" as a synonym for a "nuclear" unit consisting of parents and children. Even so, for many of us, "extended" families composed of grandparents, cousins, uncles, and aunts are a regular part of our life experience — if not in the flesh, at least in our lore. At times the boundaries of the family folk group are sufficiently fluid to admit extremely distant relatives, informally "adopted" sons or daughters, non-kin (servants, close friends, employers), and in some circumstances family pets. We include these individuals (or animals) in our family activities because, we say, "they are just like members of the family."

If folk groups are the human clusters that vitalize folklore, folklore in turn vitalizes the group by engaging its members in an ongoing informational exchange. Groups owe their stability, in part, to the *folklore forms* that contribute to their collective identity. A family that has recently emigrated from Czechoslovakia, lived through an earthquake, or suffered from the humiliation of racial prejudice is likely to codify its common experience in a set of folk expressions another family might judge inappropriate to its history and way of life.

15

Most of us know these expressions by generic names, such as "riddle," "legend," "the blues," "soul [hand] shake," "string games," "quilts," "dogtrot house," "chitterling dinner," or "blackeyed peas 'n hog jowl." As regional expressions of the Mississippi Delta culture, all could be found in circulation within a single family from that locality. Within the family group they will exist alongside specifically family-based forms such as photograph albums, home movies, family reunions, birthday parties, ancestor tales, naming traditions, and more. As participants in the folk traditions of a larger community, families have a rich folk heritage indeed.

We often hear comments such as, "Last Christmas I tried to make Mother's chocolate ice box cake, but it wasn't any good," or "Sandy's joke about 'Mr. RabBIT' is funny, but it's really his dad's story," or "Uncle Jack's version of the tale was the same as his brother Frank's except that, according to his account, the cattle Frank drove to Mexico were stolen." As part of the family's collective memory, folklore forms come to life in *performance*. To perform means to "enact" or "give shape" to something that is known but only occasionally realized. Most performances such as baking a cake or recounting a tale are individual acts. Some are so intimately associated with a single family member that other members hesitate to incorporate it into their own repertoires. However, folk expressions are usually learned from the group and re-created thereafter by several members, usually to the delight of the rest.

"No story is told the same way twice." This familiar expression means that individual talents and tastes account for variations that occur as a natural outcome of the transmission process. Basic ingredients often remain the same, but secondary features undergo frequent alteration. Stories (and cake recipes) evolve in much the same manner as dogs and cats. Cats are cats. They are also black or white, fat or thin, long- or short-haired. Likewise, the story about Frank's cattle drive may have the same characters and plot, but its performance may be comical or moralistic, spare or embellished, brief or long-winded. In time, fluid, secondary features may join the primary, permanent ones. Such evolution is entirely natural, and as with cats, subject to laws of conservation and change.

If Uncle Jack were to ring the doorbell one day and then launch directly into his cattle-drive story without removing his coat, we would probably find his behavior eccentric or odd, for performances are products of traditional and appropriate contexts. Taken together, performance and context constitute a *folk event*. These occasions are governed by considerations of time, place, participants, and motive. Calendar traditions correspond to certain dates and seasons of the year. Stories of a recently-deceased relative will, in many families, be told at his funeral or wake. In the same way, Jack could tell his story at a family meal, in a neighborhood pub, or in the car on a long journey because each context assures him of a willing audience. Often, several performances take place in a given folk event, informally or as components of a planned "script." Thus, if Jack chooses Christmas dinner as a setting for his tale, he will be in competition with a gift-exchange, egg-nog, turkey and dressing, or tales of past Christmases. Whatever their shape, folk events constitute that part of our life experience upon which the transmission of our folk heritage depends. Events, performances, folklore forms, and groups: these are the chief constitutents of the folklore process.

ORAL HISTORY? OR FOLKLORE? So far, our discussion of the folklore process has made only passing reference to the content of the material that folklore hands down. For many Americans seeking clues to their personal past, oral tradition is an important source of history. Narratives about migrations, hard times, or comic moments may be our only direct link with forebearers who came into the world, lived their lives, and passed away long ago. We may also have access to articles they left behind; portraits, clothing, weapons, houses, photographs, jewelry, and a vast array of superficially valueless objects fill in the details that narratives miss. Our reconstruction of the past, however, is generally restricted by the kind and amount of data we bring together. Memories and memorabilia may build a lavish picture of great-grandmother's teenage years, but furnish only a partial record of life after her marriage. Ultimately, behind all of this clouding material, we must sift fiction from fact. At the least, we need to establish the relative reliability of the information we have. Folklore, characterized by its inattention to verifiable fact, would seem to have little place in a search for the past. Yet recently historians have developed approaches to oral material that accommodate the dynamics of transmission and change. Today, folklore has been brought into profitable association with historical research.

Were we to examine an archives compiled by a folklorist and compare it to another assembled by an oral historian, we would find their content to be very much the same. Records would include taped accounts of personal experiences in jobs, military service, child-rearing, school, religious activities, or travels; further interviews would describe the impact on individuals generated by grand historical events; appearing, too, would be inherited group expressions such as folk beliefs, legends, tall tales, childhood rhymes, crafts, songs, poetry, whistles, handshakes, or dance steps. In asking each owner about his intentions toward this mound of data, however, we are likely to hear two radically different points of view. For whereas oral history is a record of important events and the relation of these occurrences to an individual or group, folklore is chiefly concerned with traditions which extend from the past but which reinforce values and norms that maintain groups in the present. The oral historian seeks to gain specific information about events which happened in the past in order — in so far as possible — to extract a historical truth. Folklore addresses the manner in which culturally-accepted forms give shape to an ongoing collective understanding of past experience.

In pursuing their separate goals, however, folklore and history meet at crucial points. First, folklore discloses the ways in which human groups have traditionally thought about history; second, nearly all history has been passed on in folklore forms; third, many folkloric expressions contain implicit historical references without being historically-intended.

Several years ago, Amalite Fratesi of Pine Bluff wrote down an oral story which she called the "true history" of a journey her family made from Ancona Province in Italy to a cotton plantation in the Arkansas Delta. The narrative serves two functions. It "proves" suppositions about her family origins and the motives that underlay the migration; it also "persuades" the listeners to respect their Italian heritage and accept their ethnic background as a reason for their present day success. Over the years the account has assumed the shape of dramatic legend. "Told for truth," it begins by establishing the characters, moves chronologically through a sequence of events, develops sub-stories and sub-plots, and embellishes the whole with exotic details. Historians might wish to verify the references to the *Queen Mary*, the number of passengers on board, the statement that Prince Ruspoli was the "Mayor of Italy," or Austin Corbin's "Jungle Hunt," but no one can argue with the story's historical message and its relevance to the lives of current listeners. The way people describe their history is of a piece with history. Here is how the Fratesi story begins:

This is true family history beginning in 1906. Hoping this is kept and passed on to future generations.

Ercola and Augusta Fratesi were the parents of six children, Nick-ola, (Nick); Guitano, (Guy); Geurrino, (Wine); Danelmo, (Dan); and Stellinda, (Stella); and Theraza.

Ercola and his brother, Joseppe, came to America with their families in November in 1906. The voyage was taken in a very old ship by the name of Queen Mary. It took Queen Mary one month to cross the Atlantic Ocean to New York. It was known later that it was Queen Mary's last voyage. There were 3,500 passengers on board. Over 300 were Italian immigrants. Some families settled in New Gascony, Arkansas; and others at Sunnyside, Red Leaf, Emmence, Lake Village, Hyner; all in Arkansas. Ercola and Augusta settled in New Gascony with their 6 children with 50 or 60 more Italian families to farm Mr. Gracie's land. Mr. Gracie owned 2,000 acres or more of this rich Delta land. He lived in New York. With the permission of Prince Ruspoli, Mayor of Italy, Mr. Gracie immigrated these Italian families to New Gascony...

[After losing two children to malaria, Ercola and Augusta move to

Sunnyside.]

A millionaire, Austin Corbin, who lived in New York, owned over 2,000 acres of this rich Delta land called Sunnyside. This land was worked and farmed with prisoners (Convicks). Austin Corbin while in Africa on a Jungle Hunt met a friend who told him about the Italians in Italy who were hardworkers and good farmers. They were at this time dissatisfied with high taxation and other disturbances. Hearing this, he went to Italy and contacted Prince Ruspoli. And with his permission immigrated these Italian families to Sunnyside, Arkansas, and no longer farmed with prisoners ...

The Fratesi story is historical legend in the minds of its custodians. Yet non-"true" forms such as anecdotes, jokes, or ballads may also contain a running commentary on historical and cultural facts. Their descriptions of localities, personalities, and the vicissitudes of life disclose a mood and spirit that adds a dimension of human response to the study of the past. For many years the family of former Arkansas Governor Sidney S. McMath has delighted in their father's subtly off-color tale known as "Mr. RabBIT." It is a politician's story, infused with an egalitarian spirit and a generous dose of common sense. It pokes fun at folks who "get rich quick" and then succumb to the attractions of ostentation. It also points out the inequities that result occasionally from the democratic process. Above all, it is a story about the risks people run in becoming dazzled by progress and turning their backs on the values and lessons of their cultural past:

Well, one time, a long, long time ago, there were three good, staunch, sincere, genuine friends. And they were Mr. Rabbit, Mr. Buzzard, and Mr. Turtle. And they lived in one of our deep, south counties in a deep, south state, and the land they lived on wasn't very fertile. They'd dig and scrape and barely grow enough to make a living.

So, they decided they'd get together and make themselves a truck garden. They'd grow a lucious garden with peas and beans and cabbages and make a little money. But the one thing they needed, though, for their garden to be really productive, was some fertilizer. So, they held a meeting and took a vote and sent Mr. Rabbit to Little Rock to buy them some fertilizer. He took his wheelbarrow and set on down the road. And he was gone, and he was gone, and he was gone, and he was gone. And he didn't come back, and he didn't come back, and he didn't come back.

Now, while he was GONE, Mr. Buzzard and Mr. Turtle struck oil on that poor ol' plot o' land. They struck oil and they got rich. And they built themselves a mansion and a swimming pool and had limousines...Pretty soon, here comes ol' Br'er Rabbit down the road wheelin' his wheelbarrow full of fertilizer. Lo and behold, there was that mansion with big columns and the beautiful garden with gardeners runnin' around in the yard ... but he KNEW this was the place. So, he wheeled right up to the big front door and he reached up to the big brass knocker and he knocked on the big brass knocker. The door opened. And lo and behold, there was a butler standing with a long red coat and a ruffled shirt and high button shoes ...

"Whadaya'll wont?"

"I'm just here lookin' for my friends. Where's Mr. Buzzard?"

"Well," said the butler [with a sniff], "if you want Mr. Buz-ZARD, he's down at the YARD."

"Whe ... whe ... where's Mr. Turtle?"

"Mr. TurTEL is down at the WELL."

The Rabbit took this in for a minute and then said, "Well, you tell Mr. BuzZARD out at the YARD and Mr. TurTEL down at the WELL that Mr. RabBIT is here with that great big load of SHIT!"

FORMS OF FAMILY FOLKLORE

Multiplicity. What generic label would we attach to Governor McMath's account of Mr. RabBIT? Certainly it meets the requirements of "story." At the same time, the concluding couplet rhyme contains a "joke." According to his family, the story has become a "custom" at special family dinners. Finally, it expresses a family "belief" in the dignity of the common man. Though generic terms are useful descriptive tools, they give incomplete definitions of the forms in which folklore transmission takes place. Performances are often "multiform;" they occur in several traditional forms at once. We express this idea in statements such as, "Quilts tell stories," or "Fruitcake means Christmas."

Another example of generic mix-up emerged when Sharon Houghton asked her grandmother Mamie Guest about home remedies. Mamie replied with a story that not only furnished a recipe, but provided a rationale for belief in the cure:

Her name was Bett, Bett Guest ... And they had a cousin, her name was Bell Bagley, and Bell had arthritis ... [she goes on about who was related to whom].

[Sharon]: I don't need to know the tree, the family tree, right now. I just want to know what she DID.

I got to tell you about Bell, though. IT WOULDN'T MAKE ANY SENSE IF I DIDN'T TELL YOU ABOUT BELL. Claude, her husband's name I think was Claude, they spent all their money on doctors and hospitals. And she was bedfast with arthritis. She couldn't walk. They were poor people 'cause they'd spend their money that way. And Bett, Velpo's sister-in-law, said, "I can fix up something that'll get you out of that bed." And she got some poke berry roots, poke berry, you know it has them little red berries on it, you know. And she parched it. She parched the roots, made it into a powder, and then she made a tea and gave it to Bell. And it wasn't long — Bett told her how to take it, you know — and it wasn't long 'til she got out of that bed and went to washin' clothes and cookin' and lookin' after her children. She got well, went on about her business...I don't know what proportion she took. Yeah, but Bett told her how to take it, you know. It's poison, you know, poke berry root's poison, the berries are POISON TOO. And Velpo said, "Bett," said, "Wasn't you afraid you'd kill her?"

"Naw," she said, "*She wasn't no good the way she WAS.*"

Common Types of Family Stories. A story is a verbal re-creation of past experience. A *family story* like Mamie's enshrines events that are shared by family members. They may have participated in the original experience, or they may have reached a common understanding of an event by witnessing its verbal re-creation many times. The genesis and uses of narrative in families are wide-ranging indeed. Most seem to cluster around three grand categories: tales about people (anecdotes about bosses and servants; ancestor legends; amusing character sketches), stories about dramatic or important events (sagas of dangerous encounters; life transitions such as marriage, childbirth, and death; dramatic situations as when a child gets lost or a treasure is buried and forgotten; accounts of national or racial prejudice), and reminiscenses about family responses to historic events.

Family stories vary in length and complexity. Some are short snatches that focus on a single incident; others take shape as anecdotes or sagas with full-blown characters and plot. A narrative gains emphasis and tone from its teller. His talents and taste give it a tragic, heroic, melancholy, or comic spirit. According to his purpose, he helps the story entertain, inform, soothe, or moralize. If brother Frank relates the adventures of his cattle drive as a rite of passage into manhood, his brother Jack may choose to dampen his interpretation by suggesting that, owing to naive youth, Frank never knew the cattle were stolen.

How these tales about a family past relate to a larger tradition of storytelling is an intriguing topic for investigation. Stories set against the great tapestry of human events surface occasionally from the pool of family lore, and at these times we discover how much common material family narratives share. Mody Boatright gathered several dozen midsouth versions of a family saga about a pioneer woman's lonely encounter with a wild panther.[2] In Cross County, Arkansas, Libby Woolbright heard the story again from Gertie Burnett Woolbright. The version from her family resembles those in Boatright's collection except for one detail: here, the heroine loses every stitch of her clothes:

Grandma Bell lived up in the mountains up at Witts Springs. And back in them days they did not have doctors close so women had

[2]Mody Boatright, "The Family Saga as a Form of Folklore," in *The Family Saga and Other Phases of American Folklore*, ed. Mody Boatright, et. al. (Urbana, Ill.: University of Illinois Press, 1958), pp. 130-133.

their babies at home and had midwives to come over. And that is what Granny Bell did. She was a midwife. That is why they called her Granny Bell.

Well, after her other husband died, she lived in a little house out behind Grandpa Bell and took care of him. An' he always fussed and did not want her out riding everwhere by herself because it was real dangerous. They had panthers and rattlesnakes and everything. And he always told her someday he would come home from school — he taught up there — and find out some panther had got her. But she done whatever she wanted to anyway.

Well she had this old mare and she had a side saddle, and one day she met this big panther. It happened right out there at Witts Springs, in them mountains. And, uh, so she did not know what to do but to pull her bonnet off and she threwed it down, and she kept goin' and the old mare was real slow.

She kept goin' and that thing would tear her bonnet *all to pieces* and *scream* like a woman hollering. So, after he tore up her bonnet he came after her again and when he got almost to her she threwed her apron down and he got it and stopped until he tore it in a million pieces. And he was hollerin'.

And when he got through he come after her again and by then she had figured out she could hold him off by throwin' something' down' she was wearin'. So, she threwed off her blouse and he done the same thing, but by then she was getting closer to home, so she was not so scared.

So when she got home, she drove up to the, to the, lot gate and she hollered for us to come and bring her a sheet to wrap her. She had pulled *every wrap of her clothes off* and give it to that panther 'til she could get home. And she done that down to the last piece.

And we could hear him screaming right down on the creek. Just followed her plum to the house, almost to the house. And so that is the way she saved her life. She pulled all her clothes off. I never will forget. She is settin' down there on that mare with all her clothes off. One piece at a time.

Now *that's a true story*.

In her commentary on the story, Libby reported:

When Gertie's aunt, Fannie Burnette Hinchey, heard the story on tape, she laughed and offered a bit of conservative restriction on the tale. She stated, "Gertie told a big-un." She said that the story was true, but Granny Bell had walked to "Hammer Horns to borrow something and that panther jumped out at her. When he squatted he was wide as a stand table. He could have jumped over a house." It seems that Granny had to run a mile while throwing clothes to the panther instead of riding "twenty something miles." Fannie remembered listening to Granny Bell telling the story. "I set there and listened to her. The only way she could get away from him was she tore her apron off and run for, said she run for dear life...But Gertie could not have really remembered it. She was not even born then. Well, she heard it so much, though, she just thought she remembered it."

Proverbs, Riddles, Sayings, Expressions, Words, and ... Poems? Oral tradition contains a medley of short forms. Proverbs pass on family philosophy in formulaic statements such as, "What one doesn't have in his head, he had in his feet" or "An old cat likes cheese like a young cat likes cheese." Elements of the family vocabulary may contain private words and expressions outsiders would be pressed to understand. "Yippie," "J.W.E.'s," and "Julius," are esoteric terms spoken regularly in the Johnson family.

For the Grahams of Little Rock, riddles furnish children and adults with entertainment and mental exercise. Some examples:

In walks two legs,
Carrying three legs;
Two legs sits on three legs,
Holding onto four legs.
What is it?
(A man with a three-legged stool milking a cow.)

* * *

Eight inches long and pretty good sized;
All women love it between their thighs
(Side saddle)

Sayings usually emerge from incidents or anecdotes and are thereafter used as a shorthand for the parent version. In my youth, my father would come home from a sales trip and be questioned by his father-in-law: "What did you have in the bag, boy!" The reference, I learned later, was a story about a young farmhand who stole his employer's eggs and put them in a bag to sell at market. When he returned that night with the bag still full, he explained to the surprised farmer, "No one asked what was in the bag."

Written forms also have a place in family folklore. As a child, Mary Louise Richardson composed an affectionate tongue-in-cheek verse that her mother, Amalite Fratesi, still reads to family gatherings:

My Mother

If I would tell her she is worth more than gold,
She would know that it is a lie that I have told;

If I would say that she had a husband sweet,
"Maybe," she would say, "but his stomach is bad and he can't eat
    meat."

Now if someone asked her if she liked the store,
The answer would be, "Not anymore";

23

Oh, why now? Think of all the salesmen you could meet.
"Boy, you better move faster than that if you don't want a kick in the
    seat."

Of kids, she has about four,
If she has another I know she wouldn't be sore;

Temper, oh no, she has none,
(Look out. She's not throwing that for fun!)

Now, don't think for one minute that I don't love my mother,
For, that is certain; do I have to explain any further?

Names. Our most immediate point of identification with our families is
evident in the names we bear. Their influence on our self-perception is
made clear in the way we add, shed, or transpose our names to fit new
ideas about who we are, for the gentle pressure names exert on our lives
is difficult to escape.

Naming traditions include, first of all, the repetition of given
names. Serial arrangements such as John Henry, Sr., John Henry, Jr.,
III, IV may, in everyday practice, be designated "Grandaddy John,"
"Daddy John," "Big John," "Little John." Materilineal relationships are
marked by patterns that preserve maiden, middle, or first names.

Inside family borders, nicknames or other forms of address suggest
levels of intimacy, endearment, or respect. Grandparents bear titles
such as "Nanna," "Maw Maw," "Mamaw," "Gramma," or special name
variations such as "Mama Lisa," or "Mimi." Kinship terms like "sister,"
"brother," "babe," become family nicknames. Other nicknames are important repositories for ethnic ties; for example, "Poopie" (Czech),
"Addie" (Yoruba), "Marya" (Polish). Surnames lost upon emigrating
from another country re-emerge as casual appelations or may, in time,
re-assert themselves as the official family patronymic. Abbreviations,
diminutives, embellishments, corruptions often crystalize into permanent modes of address. "John, Jr." becomes "Junior," and then "Junie;"
grandfather "Daddy Lee" undergoes a phonological transformation and
reappears as "Daddy Yee"; "Frank" becomes "Franklin," "Franklin
Wanklin," "Franklin Delano," and myriad others as family members
exercise their prerogatives as name-makers for one another.

Places and Things. In most families traditions are built from what often
seems a welter of debris, much of it isolated, fragmentary remains of the
places and props that once set the stage for family life. Letters, diaries,
journals, memoires, furniture, jewelry, samplers, quilts, clothing, and
scrapbooks are only a few examples of the stuff families collect and cling
to.

This material past, unlike narrative, is often a reference point for
loosely-structured conversations in which tangible objects — long re-
modeled, discarded, or destroyed — are revived through verbal descrip-

tion. "Grandfather Kanis installed a horse-drawn hay fork in this barn," Edwina Atkinson observed, contemplating the empty barn shell. Words explain the function of artifacts: "The ladies made this lace in the afternoons," Marguerite Henry said, "and used it for trim on their gowns and slips and things."

Material objects, real or described, are in no sense ancillary to family folklore. They bear witness to the tastes, needs, and ingenuity of ancestors by demonstrating how they dressed for church, peeled their apples, or stored their hay. In many families they are important repositories that summon up fleeting memories and anchor them briefly to the present. Together, they constitute a storehouse of family treasures — historical, sentimental, or monetary in value — that generate a sense of continuity among family members who use them over several generations.

Nearly every artifact in the family homeplace has a story. A silver teapot may have been buried in great-grandmother's back yard during the Civil War; a great-aunt's locket may have been the gift of a mysterious lover; an old shirt in a husband's drawer may mark the day you and he fell in love; a quilt great-grandmother made for you before you were born is tangible evidence of an ancestral bond. By virtue of such meanings junk is transformed into a treasure-trove.

The David Greene family, for example, has preserved an unusual collection of artifacts whose principal value resides in their power to galvanize group feelings among family members. "In looking at them," says Gaye Greene, "we see the mirror image of ourselves." A weather-beaten shingle came from the Missionary Baptist Church in Troy, Alabama, where forebears attended church around 1868. A handmade knife with an ash handle is a legacy from a great-great-grandfather and a china doll's head belonged to his wife. A prehistoric camel's tooth was an important discovery made by a great-grandfather in Texas. More recent additions include a horsehair razorstrap from grandfather, father's handmade silver ring, and a ration-book from World War II. The lore of memorabilia is plainly inseparable from its context.

Family Photographs, Albums, and Home Movies. Photographs, tintypes, and daguerrotypes kept in family attics, in photo albums, in shoeboxes, or in frames on walls tell about family traditions in several ways. By adding a visual dimension to oral remembrances, a snapshot enriches the account by filling in details that might otherwise be lost. Photos also comprise a tradition in their own right. The function of the family photographer resembles that of the family historian in the sense that he or she chronicles events by capturing them in a set of frozen "moments." Photographs, however, communicate little unless they can be identified or explained. Their merit is directly related to their meaning. For this reason, family snapshots and portraits are a helpful research tool. One of the best ways to encourage a forgetful relative is to bring out photographs that unlock significant memories. An elderly person may not only recall when the photograph was taken, but may also share other kinds of memories about people, styles, and customs which the image brings to mind.

Not all snapshots or studio portraits make their way into frames or the family album, however. Every family establishes criteria for deciding which images best reflect its collective heritage. The choice is often made by a self-appointed family photo-archivist. A careful examination of most albums will show that the image flows together in a style that gives a panoramic view of the family past. If photographs are magnets to which memories cling, it would be helpful to investigate the way events narrated through album images might influence the telling and re-telling of family tales.

Home movies give a fuller record of a single family event than snapshots can achieve. The cinematographic recording of human action is another way in which a family captures its own image over time. David Long of Little Rock explained that home movies in his family fell into two general types (1) family only, and (2) family with friends:

> The large majority of the movies were made at our house. The first type, family only, are generally of important events such as Christmas, Easter, or birthdays. The other movies also cover some of the same occasions, but are usually just pictures of my parent's friends and their children. In the movies that are of friends on special occasions, the friends are considered to be family members, and the adults were referred to as "aunt" or "uncle."

The screening of family movies creates, or is part of, a folk event:

> Movies are usually shown when all of my brothers and I are at home, and usually when my cousins and/or grandmother are there also. This is usually at Christmas. When we were younger, we saw them once during the summer and once around Christmas. We always showed a short movie or cartoon such as "Cinderella and the Silver Skates" or "Howdy Doody Christmas" before seeing family movies. This was done mainly to keep the children interested long enough to view the main attraction.

Customs and Celebrations. There are times in the course of family life when past and present seem to converge. The re-enactment of a family custom — a November chitterling dinner, for instance — is a ritualized statement about the ongoing nature of the family as an institution. Family celebrations are folk events that range in style from casual, improvised gatherings to others bound by fixed time, place, participants, and "script."

For over seventy-five years the Georgia descendants of William L. Strain (b. 1818: Lincoln Co., N.C.; d. 1896: Snake Creek Gap, Ga.) have held an annual reunion on the third Sunday in July. The event, which always takes place beside the family cemetery at Sugar Valley Baptist

Church, is composed of two parts: a noon lunch at covered picnic tables on the church grounds and an afternoon meeting held inside the church. Preparations begin long in advance. Led by officers elected the year before, volunteers remind their kinfolk of the event, write up minutes of the previous reunion, design and print a program, and calculate needed contributions to the cemetery maintenance fund.

Meanwhile, the History Committee duplicates the latest genealogical evidence of family ancestors for distribution. The "Weatherman," a traditionally elected comedian, works up a variety of disclaimers and boasts suitable to the fineness of any day. The Refreshments Committee buys cases of soft drinks, while individual family groups share assignments for food.

On the day itself, picnicking and visiting over, the business meeting begins. The 1981 meeting opened with a prayer, an introduction and welcome, hymns and "special music." Then came the "family roll call." As the name of each of the twelve William Strain offspring was announced, his or her descendants stood to be counted, as the branch "head" reported the year's marriages, births, deaths, and other important news. There were "calls," too, for "oldest in attendance," "youngest in attendance," and "the person who has travelled the furthest distance" to attend the event.

The formality does not inhibit reminiscing, the savoring of old tales and recipes, or the addition of new events to the program, such as last year's slide show of old family photographs. The "William L. Strain Family Reunion" is an old institution, a repository and at the same time a maker of history. "We need your help," pleaded last year's printed program. "Please bring your old photographs and send in your family data so we can complete our records." The Reunion is indeed a part of that record.

Family Foods. Foods are among the most enduring of family traditions. They are immortalized in stories, ritualized through customs, and naturalized from foreign sources as relished additions to family meals. They are also a matter of taste. It is reported that my great-grandmother, Julia Hamilton, was married several years before she learned what her husband meant by the cry, "Julia, this is the BEST I ever tasted!" She learned never to serve the dish again.

Foods are such entrenched habits that they are the topic of intense effort and laborious discussion. They became a central topic in a letter Jane Brown wrote her son in 1859, after he moved from Statesville, North Carolina, to Georgia:

> The white pudding you speak of is made thus: Take some suet, cut it up fine, and have some flour and rub it up together. Have a marrow bone of the beef on to boil before you begin and skim off the top to make it moist enough. Put in black pepper to season ... and salt. Stuff your entrails after you have them cleaned and prepared.

Tie the two ends together, have a pot of boiling water, and put them in to scald. Do not let them stay too long, for they burst. Take them out and hang them in a dry place and they will keep for months. When you want to rise them, put them in water and boil them like meat or anything else untill (sic) they are done. Then take them out and fry them. They are good.

After penning the recipes for "bag pudding" and "bread yeast," she concludes with a tempting bribe to her son's stomach:

I think you had better come and bring your wife with you to see me. Then I can tell her more to her satisfaction than I can write what I know by experience.

So far, the family that has inherited Jane Brown's ancestral recipes has not chosen to include them in its current cuisine.

Home Remedies. There is a close relationship between a food's capacity to nourish and a plant's power to cure. While home remedies rely chiefly on animals, insects, and "yarbs," they also depend on other curative agents such as string, mirrors, paraffin...and faith. However skeptical a scientific mind may remain in the face of grandma's cure for whooping cough, its most vital ingredient cannot be replaced: family trust and mutual concern. Here are a few Arkansas Delta remedies:

* For an earache, treat the ear with a drop of beetle blood.
* A poisonous snakebite can be cured by cutting open a black hen and tying it to the wound.
* Asafetida ("Asafidity") will relieve a stomach ache.
* A tea of mullein, sorghum, and holly leaves cures a cough.

Children's Fantasies and Games. Children are an excellent stimulus for adult imaginations and give rise to tales created expressly for the young. Story cycles about Eskimos in ice cream igloos are among tales my father created for my brothers and me when we were young. Siblings, too, create worlds out of dolls, string games, songs, and dramas with imaginary friends. Their existence may be short-lived, but their remembrance has a profound impact on family solidarity and traditions.

A second "panther" story from the Woolbright family begins a traditional scare game played in late evening by firelight. The teller is Gertie Burnette Woolbright:

One time there was this old lady, and she lived by herself, way back in the back woods, and she would get so lonesome. And one night it was real bad and stormy, and she went to the door and she said, "Who is going to stay with me this dark and stormy night?" And a voice from way over in the woods somewhere said [in a high-pitched, distant tone], "IIII wiiill."

She went back and she rocked and she smoked and rocked and smoked, and she went back to the door and she said, "Who is going to stay with me this dark, stormy night?" Something a bit closer said, "IIIII wiiill."

She went back and smoked and rocked, and she rocked and smoked, and she went back to the door and she said, "Who is going to stay with me this dark, stormy night?" And something right out, right out, in the lot says, "I will."

So, she went back again, and every time it was getting a little closer, and a little closer. So she went back and sat back down and she smoked and rocked. And she went back to the door and she said, "Who is going to stay with me this dark, stormy night?" Something just outside the door said, "I WILL." So, she went back and she sat down again, and when she went back this last time, something [understood: panther] well, grabbed her and ATE HER UP! [Gertie lunges for the children, who squeal with delight.]

Family Beliefs. Families share with their larger culture a set of ideas about the ways people behave in society and about what is possible in the natural world. Ewing family lore pins predictions on parts of the body:

If your right eyelid jumps, something glad will happen.

If your left eyelid jumps, you will become annoyed.

If your right eye jumps at the same time as your left eye, you will be lucky.

If your right ear rings, you will receive good news.

If your left ear rings, you will receive bad news.

If you sweep a lady's feet, it means you will walk on strange ground.

If you step over a child, you will stop his growth.

The first person coming through your door on New Year's Day must be male.

If your lips itch, "someone is lying about you."

If a bird builds his nest with your hair, you will go crazy.

FAMILY FOLKLORE AND THE COMMUNITY. Families absorb traditions and tales from their localities and in turn contribute their own lore to the network of traditions shared by neighbors and friends nearby. In Arkansas quilting bees have entertained women, their daughters, and daughters-in-law for generations; in many, participation is obligatory with family membership. Similarly, a family-owned store may be the center of community life. Tales spun over the stove or outside the back door pass in and out of family groups, heedless of national or racial boundaries. Beadie Estelle Johnson of Marianna heard this anecdote from her husband, proprietor of a general mercantile store. It is likely that the punchline was originally spoken as a wry, indirect comment on the collection and transportation of day-laborers to rural farms:

There was two old nigras. I'll call one of 'em Will and the other'n Jim. And [my husband] said they were old and poor and they'd come and sit there [by the stove] to keep warm and maybe get some cheese and crackers to eat for their lunch. And he just couldn't keep from listenin' to 'em. Said they had a revival goin' on and said this ol' Jim

29

said to Will, said, "Will, you been takin' in that revival?"

"Yeah, man, didn't you see me?"

He said, "Yeah, I thought I saw you, but I didn't know." Said, "When that preacher said all of dem wanna go to Heabm hol' up der han, why didn' yo hol' up yo han'?"

He said, "'Cause I thought it'd be sech a big load, I wanted to go on the *second* load!"

Our investigation goes on. Any inventory of the forms that encapsulate and transmit the folklore of American descent groups is unlikely to be complete. To the foregoing list we might add dance steps, folk art, musical traditions, family hobbies and avocations, funerals and wakes, prayer meetings, musical traditions, family businesses, and many more. In the next chapters, seven families share their traditions. These examples and descriptions contain images of lives led in the Arkansas Delta ... and on its edge. They are lives that interweave — in agriculture, in commerce, and in the passing down of regional lore.

—Deirdre La Pin

The Johnson-Dixon Family
Going "All The Way 'Round By Laura's House"

Stephanie Dixon was talking about her father Bob Johnson in Marianna. "A grocery store is his main thing, but he and his daddy farmed...Oh!" A bright flash lit her face. "That's a story! I've got to tell you the 'Bull' story. You can help me out with it," she commanded her husband Bill. "I think it was the year I graduated from high school. The superintendent of schools asked Daddy..." "Here we go," Bill chimed, "All the way 'round by Laura's house." "Yes," Stephanie agreed, "All the way 'round by Laura's house." And with this formula, as always, a long family tale begins (see "The Bull Story," pg. 34).

Tales: A Family Tradition. Barnyard animals, friends, family past and present are the figures out of raw experience that imaginative families like the Johnsons redraw over the years into heroes for their domestic tales.

Some observers would suggest that the Johnson storytelling tradition should be traced eastward through the southern migrations routes, back to the British soil from which it grew. Stephanie's forebears on her father's side — the Johnsons from Virginia, the Jeffcoats from South Carolina, the McGrews and the Suitts — wended their way through Alabama and Mississippi where they met her mother's ancestors — Allens, Edwardses, Parkes and others — who had followed a similar trail. By the outbreak of the Civil War the Johnsons, McGrews and Allens had settled in Lee County, Arkansas, while the Edwardses and Parkes lingered in Mississippi, working as merchants, farmers, and justices of the peace. Trades were important to the family; A. B. Suitt was a carriagemaker, Samuel Johnson a blacksmith, and in 1912 great-great-grandmother Edwards put down two dollars to become the first Avon Lady in Mississippi.

The Bull Story_____

(Stephanie tells the story to Deirdre and husband Bill):

There's a man in Marianna named Geether King, G. O. King, who buys and sells livestock. And he had a bull on the other end of town that Daddy and Gary bought. And...uh...they bought this bull one morning, and...uh...none of the women in the family knew about it. Of course, they carry on their business and maybe two weeks later one might say, "Oh, yeah, we bought a bull."

Well, Camille [Stephanie's sister] and the wife of the Sheriff had gone to Memphis. Well, the Sheriff is Camille's husband's cousin; his name is Bobby May. So Camille and the Sheriff's wife go to Memphis and the men buy this bull and bring him from across town.

Well, the bull missed his harem on the other end of town, so he proceeds to tear down a fence and make his way back across town to this other farm. My dad's property abuts the golf course. [Everyone laughs.] The bull goes across the golf course chasing people...clubs going everywhere! (More laughter.) He gets down to the L'Anguille River, which he wades. It's called a river, but it's just a glorified CREEK.

(Bill: A MOSQUITO sanctuary!)

(Deirdre laughing.)

Anyhow, he comes up there, and he comes down this little road which passes the cemetery...they're having a funeral (GIGGLING)...and then he comes up into TOWN up to where the courthouse is.

Well, by this time, the phone has been ringing off the Sheriff's wall ... "There's a BULL loose! He's come across the river. He's scaring all the fishermen and the golfers..." and Bobby is just having a fit about where the bull is and how he's going to catch it. And by this time he knows that it's Gary's.

Well, Camille and Peggy get back into town, and Camille takes Peggy back to the courthouse so she can ride home with Bobby, and as she drives up...there's a BULL runnin' up the courthouse steps!

(Deirdre is laughing hard.)

Well, now the courthouse sits on top of...the ONLY hill in Marianna, and the steps are pretty steep. It's not something that you could MISS. So Camille runs in the courthouse screaming, "Bobby! There's a bull loose ... " Bobby interrupts and says (irritably), "I know! And it's YOURS." She says, "I don't have a bull." "Yes, you do!" So at this point he says, "Where's the bull?" And she says (innocently), "I don't know, but...uh...why don't you go stand around in front of the courthouse. You can probably SEE him from there." (Stephanie is laughing so hard she can hardly finish.)

(Bill and Deirdre are laughing, too.)

So the next thing she sees is the Sheriff running back around the corner of the courthouse. He has SPOTTED the bull. But before they could get somebody to catch him, he gets all the way across town, into the pasture where he started originally. And at that moment Daddy said, "This is enough."

We sold the bull back to Geether King. They owned the bull ONE DAY.

"Great storytellers on both sides," Stephanie observes, the family has passed down its talent and traditions for nearly two hundred years. A well-established family story is fairly easily discerned. If much-used, it will emerge as a tidy mixture of characters, setting, and plot, all arranged by repeated honing against many tellers' skills. But if still young, that is, fresh from experience or relatively unshared, it pursues a much rougher course. It may leap uncontrollably from one episode to another without heed to a story line; it may balance a beginning against the middle but run out of steam near the end; or it may make a poor selection of points, too many or too dull, and tire the listener's will to make sense of the whole. Because the chief purpose of storytelling among the Johnsons is to promote family closeness, any new story, however flawed, is greeted the first time by an eager audience. If it brings pleasure, it will surely be retold, and as its wrinkles gradually disappear, it passes into the permanent family repertoire.

Whether tidy old or untidy new, most of the stories the Johnsons tell promise a comic situation rich in detail and nearly tripping over itself in a headlong dash from one scene to the next ... and the next ... and the next. If the tales are long and complex more often than short, it is because their business is to share the past. Not, as many might suppose, by merely telling *about* something that happened, but by reproducing an event with such fullness that it gives the impression of happening once again. A gifted storyteller can resurrect the past even more vividly by adding to his task as narrator the impersonation of character parts. Voice, face, hands, and torso translate into the present the words, actions, and feelings of the past. Stephanie's demeanor changes suddenly during the "Bull" story when she describes sister Camille spotting the bull downtown: "As she drives up ... there's a bull runnin' up the courthouse steps!" At that moment Camille sits where Stephanie once was; her eyes grow large, her face is transfixed by surprise, her body contracts in a forward thrust, and her voice is high with anxiety. Such a story sends the listener's imagination hurtling down the story trail in hot pursuit of Camille and the bull. And indeed every time the storyteller turns a bend to open up a new stretch of road, the listener mentally tightens his hold on the flow of words. "What," he wonders, "will happen next?" By the time the audience is hopelessly enmeshed in Camille's experience, Stephanie has achieved her aim: for a moment she has induced them to leave the present and to follow her on a journey into the past. They have, together, gone "all the way 'round by Laura's house."

This formula has been in Stephanie's family since at least the time of her two grandmothers. No one can remember hearing it used by anybody outside the family, though its presence in both the Johnson and Allen branches suggests an external origin. The saying is cherished because it sums up certain communal ideas about stories, storytelling, and the ongoing recollection of the family past.

To go "all the way around," first of all, underscores the importance of completeness in the telling, for the Johnsons enjoy savoring each other's experiences to the full. Stephanie put it this way: "You're telling a long involved story and instead of going in a straight line you say, 'Well, I'm going all the way 'round by Laura's house.'" The announcement, which usually comes at the beginning, sends a signal to the audience that a lengthy and entertaining saga is in store. Be patient, it says, and don't expect the story to make its point in a hurry.

Secondly, on a more intuitive level, "Laura's house" stands as a metaphor for a place somewhere outside actual place and time. It beckons the listener to make an imaginative leap into another world, a world that comprises a past. Johnson narratives compose a remarkable legacy spanning a period from the Revolutionary War to the events of yesterday (see Family Ancestor Stories, p. 40). It is unlikely that this world would square exactly with historical facts, but such measures of accuracy are almost beside the point. More relevant is the constant dynamic the stories effect between who the Johnsons were in the past, are in the present, and expect to be in the future. Families, like communities and nations, perpetuate their oral traditions, not because they are impartially reliable records, but because they can be deliberately shaped to reinforce specific behaviors, values, and ideas. If history makes stories, it is equally true that stories make history. The Johnson zeal for revisiting the past and reliving its events is thus bound up with a larger passion. That passion is the family itself: its physical presence, its mutual love, its fervent solidarity. It is a theme that underpins every facet of the family's self-expression, what we call here, its folklore.

Stories are only a part of the Johnson-Allen folklore heritage. Names ("Sudie" and "Big Daddy"), festivals (Christmas and fall chittlin' suppers), and food ("Mammy's famous rolls" and "true ambrosia") are regular features of the family's communal life. Women are the chief tradition-bearers. One reason is that most gatherings center around food, and the women preside over the kitchen and meals. But a more important reason is that, in Stephanie's words, they've "lived so long and bred so fast."

Names. Five generations of women are living today in Stephanie's family through a direct line of female descent. Over this unofficial matriliny reigns Sudie Lee Edwards (remarried Belew), a great-great-grandmother of ninety-four years. Outsiders may consider her and her daughters to be Edwardses (or Belews), Allens, Johnsons, and Dixons, but if naming is a mark of kinship, then Mama Belew and her female forebears understood that first names are an equivalent blood-binding domain. With the birth of Sudie Lee Yates in 1842, a naming tradition preserved "Sudie" in each generation down to the present. The first Sudie named her eldest daughter "Sudie Eliza," who in turn passed the name on to her daughter "Sudie Lee." Intervention of other family

Stephanie Dixon's great-great-grandmother Sudie Eliza Yates was descended from the family of Colonel Robert Bolling and his second wife Anne Stith. His first wife was Jane Rolfe, daughter of John Rolfe and Pocahontas. This engraving from the Yates family files is reproduced from *Memories of the Bolling Family*, "written by John Bolling of Chellowe, Buckingham County, Virginia, translated from the original French manuscript by John Robertson, Jr., son of Wm. 1603."

members (see p. 38) prevented this Sudie, today's Mama Belew, from choosing that name for her daughter Willie Mae; but the family relishes the tale of how, at the age of sixty-five, she took the matter in her own hands and assigned "Sudie" to herself. "I was the only generation they missed," she explained. On her birth certificate, her new name appears "Willie Mae Sudie Lee Eloise Edwards." Even so, the family continues to call her by the nickname her father preferred: "Bill."

"Sudie" survives in modern times, though it has given way to the modern variant, "Sue." Its persistence reflects an implicit family rule grounded in long experience with maternal authority and strong female ties. The tradition contrasts squarely with other family branches which pass down only male names, from father to son. "In every other branch," Stephanie remarked, "they named one of the sons for the father, except for my uncle Jess, but his name is Jess Paul Odom, and he has a son Paul Douglas Odom, who has a son Jess Douglas Odom!"

Parallel to naming traditions are those acknowledging the relationships between family members. Kinship terms — "Daddy," "Auntie," Gramps," "Nanna," and the like — could arguably be said to have many properties of nicknames when they are attached to a single person — "Daddy Jim," "Auntie Jane," and so on. But when they are used generally, they work as titles that pass from one generation to the next. The multiple generations in Stephanie's family yield so many sets of relationships that titles sometimes turn into nicknames in order to avoid reduplication. Eight generations ago, "Bill" Allen recalls, the family adopted "Mammy" and "Big Daddy" as affectionate titles for her grandparents. Later, when "Bill's" children were born, her parents took the names until grandchildren came, and then she and her husband

"Bill" Allen Changes Her Name_____

(Bill, talking to her granddaughter Stephanie)

B: Uncle Will was the one wanted to name me Willie Mae.

S: He was the one that delivered you, wasn't he?

B: Yeah. And they had had a little girl named Willie Mae. This was their oldest child.

S: Uncle Will and Aunt Mae were married.

B: Yeah. And she died a year or two before I was born. They called it congestion. ... Well, I had always disliked the name and made the mistake of saying so one time in Aunt Mae's presence. And she said, "You mean you don't really like your name?" and I said, "No m'm." Cause I never was one to tell...I mean I told it like it was. So I always felt like I should have been named Sudie Lee, not that I especially liked "Sudie," but I think Lee is a beautiful name. I love it. *But because it's a family name and I was the only generation they missed....* Well, then it was time to get my birth certificate ... I decided that this was the time I could get my name settled. I could name myself. And Mama signed an affidavit that it was true. And I named myself Willie Mae Sudie Lee Eloise Edwards. Mama had always wanted to name me Eloise, so I added that to the other stuff.

assumed the part. The titles were traditional, but some family members accused her of usurpation. Her argument was simple: "I said, 'Listen, I'm not doing that to take anything away from THEM [her parents]; it's because I think every child ought to have a Mammy and a Big Daddy.'" But there, "Bill" admits, the title stuck. When her daughter Shirley said she would like HER grandchildren to call her Mammy, the family agreed "they already had one."

(Far left) Sudie Lee Yates.
(Middle) Sudie Eliza Yates Parkes and
to the left is the twin Sudie Parkes
Edwards, remarried Belew. (Right)
"Mama Belew" with Willie Mae Sudie
Lee Eloise Edwards to the right.

The Edwards Heirs. "Lost fortune" stories are found in the permanent repertoire of nearly every family. The Edwardses' favorite involves land in Manhattan that was lost through illegal sale. Stephanie remembers hearing as a child that "the family owned a lot of land in Manhattan that was taken away from us, and I remember something about the Civil War, that they lost it through the Civil War, that since then they've been trying to — not get the land back — but to get some sort of money for it, to have the claim recognized in some way."

The evidence is found in a stack of large file folders jammed with Xeroxed documents which passed to Stephanie from a distant Edwards cousin in Texas. The files contain letters, newspaper articles, a New York State Assembly bill, minutes from meetings of The Edwards Heirs Association, maps of lower Manhattan, an appellant's brief to the New York Supreme Court, and a notice of indictment for fraud against a general manager of Descendants of Thomas Hael (Hall), Inc.

What makes this story noteworthy is its power to fire the family's collective "determination" numerous times over more than a century in an epic and legal battle over a real estate claim valued from ten million to four billion dollars. The chief perpetrator of this villainy, the legend contends, was Manhattan's Trinity Church, across from Wall Street at Broadway. Numerous versions of the story are recorded in Stephanie's files, and their divergent and often conflicting accounts furnish a graphic example of the interplay between family legend, written history, and the continuous quest for instant wealth.

According to a turn-of-the-century southern version, the family involvement began when Robert Edwards from England and Thomas

39

LEMACH EDWARDS (1794-1861): His Famous Temper

It's been a tradition in the family that when a kid throws a big temper tantrum, they say, "He has Lemach's temper."

He would get into a fit, and after he had finished destroying whatever it was he was destroying, he would go into the buggy and sulk. And they would leave him out there overnight or maybe a day or two until they thought he was calm enough. His wife Nancy would go out there to see if he was calm. She was the only one who could do anything with him...that's how my grandmother put it. And then they'd welcome him back into the family.

DR. BILLY EDWARDS (1807-1916): "A dentist, merchant, and cockfighter in Sturgis, Mississippi; not necessarily in that order. Civil War veteran." (When on a visit to Sturgis, Stephanie asked an old man if he knew Dr. Billy, he said, "Yes! He pulled many of my teeth!"

He said there was an old black man, and if you wanted your teeth pulled you would go to the back of the store and there was a chair. This black man was named Sam. And when he [Dr. Billy] gave Sam the signal...he winked or did something...Sam would reach around behind you and GRAB you, and he would yank the tooth! And you never knew it was coming.)

GRANDMAW AND GRANDPAW YATES (she, 1842-1915): "Bill" Allen tells the story of their cooking contest.

In OUR family the women always did the cookin'. But Grandpaw Yates, Mammy's [her grandmother's] father, made some kind of brick oven-like thing. He decided he was going to have all kinds of wild game, he was going to cook it in this thing and have all his friends over to eat. He was going to seal the door and cook it, you know. Well, Grandma was just upset no end; she said wadn't anything be fit to eat, he couldn't invite all those people.

Well, of course in those days there was every kind of wild animal you could think of to eat, including turkeys and quail. So he said he was going to do it — he was one of those kind of men — and he was going to fix it anyway. So Grandmaw went back to the kitchen off from the house, she went back there and she started cooking roast beef, chickens, hens, and I don't know what all...she just cooked up a storm. Well, finally the time came to unseal the door and have the meal. And Mammy says it was the most delicious food that you ever ate in your life... that HE had cooked. And that SHE had cooked, too! (Laughter)

MAW MAW AND PAW PAW (1892-1971; 1897-): How they got married.

My grandfather Johnson (Paw Paw) was seventeen when he was married, and she was fourteen. Her father was apparently a REAL difficult man, Mr. McGrew. She had nothing but good things to say about him, but he was definitely an old hill man. He was in his fifties when she was born. And she was just a baby.

Well, she and my grandfather decided to get married, and they ran off. And my grandfather used to tell me that the old man got SO MAD that he was just furious, that he was going to kill him!

And my grandmother and granddaddy moved into a house that was about a mile away from where her parents lived. And my granddaddy rode a mule to work every day and had to ride past that house. And he said no matter how early he got up in the morning to ride that mule, my grandmother's daddy was sitting out on the porch in the rocking chair with a gun across his lap. And he said he

NEVER KNEW when he passed by when he was gonna hear a gunshot that would be the last thing he ever heard. And no matter how late he came back home in the evening, there he was with the gun across his lap.

But after this had gone on about a month, her mother sent word that they were to come over for chicken, and everything was okay after that. Apparently the daddy thought, "If he's got nerve enough to go to work every day and me sitting here pointing this gun at him, then he must be all right."

Edwards from Wales came to Manhattan in the 1740s. Twenty years later, England's King George III granted both men extensive holdings in Manhattan. When the Revolutionary War ended, Thomas Edwards' sons made a ninety-nine year lease of their father's property to Trinity Church. Time passed, their descendants joined the trek west and south, and the lands were never returned.

Meanwhile, the northern Edwardses were resting their claim on a yet earlier arrival, one Thomas Hael or Hall, who in two deeds dated 1642 was granted certain Hudson River lands known as "Lot 5" on the Maerschalk Map of Manhattan. When Thomas Edwards married Hael's daughter and only heir Elizabeth, a third deed dated 1673 passed the title to him. Today Lot 5 adjoins Trinity Church, but so far, no document has been found to prove that ownership was legally conveyed to the Church Corporation. The only clue is a much later lease showing that a Robert Edwards in 1778 deeded seventy-seven acres of land to John and George Cruger for ninety-nine years. Were the Crugers acting on behalf of Trinity Church? Some expanded versions of the legend assume that they were. More important, is this Robert the same adventurer who crossed the Atlantic some thirty years earlier? How are the two versions to be reconciled?

If the northern and southern accounts appear as only shadowy reflections of one another, an important reason is that each takes a different approach to story making. One pins its account on facts drawn from written sources; the other relies chiefly on oral tradition. But it was for the same reason that Edwardses everywhere were re-telling history: it was to prove either to the courts, to other heirs, or to themselves that the family had been tricked out of its rightful inheritance by a powerful religious corporation. From the 1890s onward the Edwards Heirs launched and maintained a succession of associations dedicated to the "Cause." Offices sprang up in Birmingham (Alabama), New Orleans, Greenville (South Carolina), Indianapolis, Atlanta, and New York City under The Descendants of Thomas Hall (Hael), Inc.; Hall-Edwards Properties, Inc.; The Genealogy Research Bureau, Inc. and more.

By the 1930s, the Allen branch of the Edwards family (Stephanie's grandparents) was only one of a reported five thousand families from Manhattan to Norfolk Island in the South Pacific solidified by Edwards genealogists into a determined, fighting force. To the battle they contributed not only their funds, but their independent variations of the family legend which, once in circulation, heightened the momentum of the "Cause." How much these tales genuinely reflect any family's vision of the past is impossible to know from the papers in Stephanie's files, but the documents make plain that what these accounts lacked in orthodoxy they gained in a persuasive power to galvanize the extended Edwards family into action.

One gifted raconteur was W. T. Edwards, whose presidential address to the Edwards Heirs in 1924 swelled the southern version into a grand drama of treachery and romance by drawing upon familiar folk characters of America's past. In the 1750s the French and Indian Wars were in full revival when Robert and Thomas (here they are brothers) disembarked in Manhattan. Thomas joined the battle, and the Indians showed their gratitude for his valiant service with a handsome option on 5,000 acres of land. On his death, the administration of the estate passed to Robert, his oldest son. The family, however, had debts, and the young man chose a ruinous course to restore financial solvency: he offered a ninety-nine year lease (without right of sublease) to Aaron Burr. "A dainable heresy," President Edwards thundered, as he traced Burr's first illegal sublease to Trinity Church and his second to New York's First Presbyterian Church; eventually, the land passed to both institutions in perpetuity without the participation of the legal owners.

Burr's reputation for infamy could not fail to raise the Edwards' ire, and in some cases to loosen the strings on their pocketbooks. As it turned out, the story ended with W. T. Edwards himself playing the traitor's part. Minutes to an Association meeting dated February 5, 1926, record accusations of incompetence, embezzlement, and other actions "injurious to the Cause of Edwards Heirs." Edwards denied the charges but resigned as President. In taking small amounts of money from persons believing themselves to be heirs, Edwards confirmed a pattern initiated in the 1890s by other leaders of the movement, especially the disreputable H. W. Ingersoll, who wrote to W. T. Edwards in 1893, "I think we have found the door which if opened to us will reveal all about this estate with one thousand millions in New York City alone."

This pattern pushed Edwards claims to such a fever pitch that in 1931 Franklin D. Roosevelt, then governor of New York, issued a statement reconstructed by the *New York Times*: "There had never been a Robert Edwards — at least not a Robert Edwards who had amassed an $850,000,000 fortune and owned the Empire State Building, the Woolworth Building, the ground in Washington on which the White House is built and forty precious acres of Manhattan."

By the Fifties it was plain that even a great statesman could not end what family legend had begun. Though traditional and oral, legends are "told for truth;" they invite belief and for this reason persist alongside published data as evidence in court and legislative documents relating to the Edwards claim. Even the northern Edwardses departed from their insistence on written records by inviting the New York Supreme Court to consider an appellant's brief including an oral narrative under the bold rubric "Statement of Facts": "Back in the early 1600's when New York was still New Amsterdam and in Dutch hands, a British fleet anchored at night and out of gunshot near Staten Island. They were prepared to launch a surprise attack on the Dutch the following morning. During the night one of the men from the fleet swam or rowed ashore and gave the Dutch news of the impending attack which enabled them to repell it. In gratitude for this deed the Dutch gave the informer a piece of land on Manhattan Island, and it is this land which the Edwards family claims. The man's name was Thomas Hall (Hael) ... "

The Edwards legend was the main force behind a New York State Assembly bill introduced in 1950, which sought the creation of a temporary state commission to investigate Trinity Church's dominion over property deeded originally to Thomas Hall (Hael). Legislators argued that private ownership of the lands would open additional sources of tax revenue; the Edwards Heirs welcomed the bill as a confirmation of their claim. Not surprisingly, the outcome of the "Cause" in the Fifties merely reinforced the pattern established decades earlier. The Post Office Inspector ruled that Edwardses across the nation had been ensnared in a plot to defraud them of funds. The "dainable heresy" had risen from within their own ranks.

"For truth" or "for fraud" the variant legends of Edwards Heirs can be seen with hindsight to have served a triple purpose. As records of history, they rekindled the memory of a traditional claim; as a focus for belief, they knit the separate Edwards families into a single unit bound to a cause; as part of the Edwards experience, they offer a tantalizing source of speculation and a fund of mixed delight. Mythical bonanza perhaps, but Stephanie would say: I hope we cash in!

Family Festivals. In their everyday lives, the members of Stephanie's family interact in many ways, and these functions require a remarkable variety of roles. Stephanie is the family planner, counselor, wage-earner, historian; Bill is the family carpenter, travel-agent, accountant, and wage-earner (his occupation, railroad switchman, was passed down from his father); Grandma Shirley is the gardener; Mammy is the master chef; Great Aunt Edith is the family archivist. But on occasions when "being together," and not a routine task, is the motive behind family communion, a more particularized set of roles comes into play. A jovial spirit usually pervades these events, and so they may rightly be called "family festivals." These get-togethers bear witness to the dynamics of kinship by reaffirming the ongoing reality of family through time. Whether motivated by religion (Christmas or Easter), by rites of passage (funerals, weddings, christenings), by national spirit (Thanksgiving, the Fourth of July), or by family custom (family reunions), these festivals are repeated events that lift the participants out of everyday experience and project them into the realm of family memory. "The one thing I remember as much as anything else," said Stephanie's Aunt Willa Stein, "are the times that we spent together."

Chittlin' suppers were, until very recently, "a sort of family reunion" in the Johnson family around hog-killing time. These gatherings developed spontaneously about thirty years ago when the family was living in La Grange. Maw Maw Johnson recalls that, when she was a girl, chitterlings were a regular part of her family diet. "I can't remember the day," she remarked, "that we didn't butcher our own meat." As the chitterlings began to disappear from the dinner table, the taste for them remained. Preparations for the big supper would begin two or three days in advance. Twenty or thirty pounds of chitterlings "stump slung and hand flung" (in other words, very fresh) were cleaned, soaked for a day in brine, and washed five or six times until they were perfectly white. Then the intestines were put in two large kettles and boiled on electric hotplates set out in the yard. Frying was the master touch. Maw Maw's chitterlings were "not floppy" but crisp and golden brown. "Everybody was chicken if they didn't come," remarks Aunt Willa Stein. Maw Maw's four children, fourteen grandchildren, and her many great-grandchildren would be joined by assorted in-laws as they sat down to a meal of salad, french fries, vegetable and bean salad ... and chittlin's. "We didn't care if we didn't have anything else," Willa Stein declared, but for squeamish in-laws pork chops or steak were supplied. Today, these suppers are a vivid memory in the family, and Maw Maw's grandsons ply her yearly with ardent requests for another. But the effort is too great for her now, and the festival awaits another chitterling enthusiast to take charge.

The Johnson chittlin' supper illustrates the way festivals resemble plays; for it is generally true that their celebration follows a script which has been handed down from the past. Every family member contributes to the script over the years by inventing a personal part that reflects his talents, interests, or position in the family structure. These plays, then, are somewhat different from their literary counterparts in the sense that they depend wholly upon their actors for re-creation and survival. Furthermore, the plays change with their parts. If a family member dies or moves away, for example, his part is altered, either because it is filled

---

An Infant's Game _____

Stephanie: One of the games we always use with the babies is to teach them different parts of the body:

Forehead-Bender, Eye-Winker;	(Touching forehead and eye)
Tom-Tinker, Nose-Dropper;	(Touching skull and nose)
Mouth-Eater, Chin-Chopper;	(Touching mouth and chin)
And Gitchee, Gitchee, Gitchee.	(Tickling neck)

Paisley loved that. Erin did, too.

Five generations: a typical family pose. (Seated) Mama Belew, (clockwise to her left) Willie Mae "Bill" Edwards, Shirley Johnson, Stephanie Dixon, Erin Dixon.

by someone else, deleted from the script, or — as in Maw Maw's case — unfilled, preventing the production of the play.

To cancel a Christmas or Easter festival would to most families be unthinkable, but their scripts naturally undergo upheaval when principals pass from the scene. Christmas in the extended Johnson family has always begun on December sixteenth, the date of Beadie Estelle (Maw Maw) Johnson's birthday. A non-relative might view this an illogical point to begin, but to the family "It's mostly her birthday, but it's Christmas, too." The "Christmasy feeling" prevails during the trimming of the tree and readying of gifts, reaching full expression when the food preparations begin. For the Bob Johnsons, Maw Maw's and Mammy's ("Bill" Allen's) households were the original centers of the feast. The grandparents' homes are located close by, the paternal family across the street and the maternal family a mile away in Marianna town.

Until ten years ago, Christmas followed an unchanging routine. Around seven o'clock on Christmas Eve, Maw Maw's children and grandchildren would collect at her house around the tree, snacking, talking, and playing games. Above the din, the crackle of fireworks could be heard from the yard. "We had sparklers, Roman candles," Stephanie recalls, "more than on the Fourth of July." The highlight of the evening was marked by the arrival of a Santa Claus, who passed out candy canes to the children with stern warnings that they'd better get to bed if they wanted any gifts! The cousins sank into the beds and mattresses Maw Maw arranged throughout the house, while Bob's children returned to their own beds across the street. Freed of the sleeping children, the aunts and uncles caroled around the neighborhood until midnight and then returned home to frantically prepare the toys before waking the children at two o'clock. A telephone call across the street synchronized events in both households. After the gifts were unwrapped, the whole group reassembled for a big breakfast at Maw Maw's where they bid good bye to Aunt Willa Stein and Uncle Jess, who hurried off to reach his parents in Ruston, Louisiana, by noon.

Later that morning, the feast entered its second phase at the Allens. More gifts preceded a traditional noon meal: boiled ham, roast turkey, sweet congealed salads, tomato aspic, candied sweet potatoes, assorted pies, fresh coconut cake, and always ambrosia. To Mammy Allen, ambrosia was the symbolic core of the meal because the original recipe ("true ambrosia," she calls it) was handed down from Mammy Parkes more than a hundred years ago. Then, it consisted only of oranges and fresh coconut, but more recently Mammy added pineapple and whipped cream. Her family's attention, however, is today fixed on another component, known affectionately as "Mammy's famous rolls." It is a family joke that they are never served without the disclaimer: "These aren't fit to eat; they're *gummy!*"

"It was just too much," Stephanie says of the old Christmas, "because we were having seventy-five people at Maw Maw's house ... We still get together a couple of times a year, everybody. But as far as Christmas goes, everyone is in their own little family group now." Today the re-creation of the festival, as it must, is falling to the younger generation; but, so far, the transition is incomplete. A family's collective memory does not easily give up old scripts, even when the actors who made them seek to retire. The spirit of Christmas present is indeed

---

Gary The Horse Trader

Stephanie: Gary [her brother-in-law] is an entrepreneur.

Deirdre: Oh, he's a horse trader.

Bill: He could sell an ice box to an Eskimo. I'll tell you a story about Gary. It's my *favorite* story. Absolutely.

Gary once bought a horse. Well, he had this horse and a man in Marianna decided that he wanted to buy a horse for his daughter. So he came out and looked at the horse that Gary had and agreed to buy it. Paid him $125. But he didn't have any place to keep it 'cause he lived in town. He asked Gary if Gary would keep the horse there. And he'd give him $15 a month to pay for the horse's food and look after the horse and let the little girl come out and ride it whenever she could.

Well, after six months she'd ridden the horse three times. She was scared of it. And he decided he didn't want the horse any more. So Gary bought the horse back from him for $100.

He sold the horse for $125 and kept it for six months for $15 a month, which was $90. And he bought it back for $100. So he took in $215 and paid back $100. So, he made $115 on the horse, and the horse never set foot out of the lot.

"Mammy" Willie Mae holding another tin of "Mammy's Famous Rolls."

charged with the spirit of Christmas past. And yet a festival is never static. Its momentum arises from fresh elements as much as from the old ones. Even so, major revisions are deeply felt. Usually a new play evolves through several years of rehearsal-like attempts until the actors settle into their roles, grow used to their props, and agree on the order of events. Meanwhile, in the Dixon family, Santa Claus still comes to Maw Maw's house on Christmas Eve, and when Bill Dixon can get off work, he and Stephanie bring the children from Little Rock. Mammy still provides rolls and ambrosia wherever the Christmas meal is held. The Bob Johnsons still have a starlight Christmas and morning breakfast, although Uncle Jess no longer leaves for Ruston at dawn. But however the new scripts are written, it is a foregone conclusion that each will preserve many traditional features, features that go "all the way round by Laura's house."   —Deirdre LaPin

PEDIGREE CHART

DATE
NAME **Stephanie Dixon**
STREET ADDRESS 5225 Melbrook
CITY North Little Rock, ARK. 72118
STATE

1. Stephanie Dixon

2. **Robert Truman Johnson**
   BORN July 18, 1918
   WHERE Lee Co., Ark.
   WHEN MARRIED Dec. 1945
   DIED
   WHERE

3. **Shirley Eloise Allen**
   BORN Oct. 1, 1925
   WHERE Lee Co., Ark.
   DIED
   WHERE

4. **Floyd Lafayette Johnson**
   christened Samuel Floyd
   BORN June 1892
   WHERE 106 Tigh, Lee Co. Ark.
   WHEN MARRIED Jan. 1, 1971
   WHERE Lee Co.
   DIED

5. **Beadie Estelle McBrew**
   BORN Dec. 1897
   WHERE White Co.
   DIED
   WHERE

6. **George Henry Allen**
   BORN 11-14-1902
   WHERE Lee Co. Ark.
   WHEN MARRIED March 1974
   DIED
   WHERE Lee Co.

7. **Willie Mae (Bill) Edwards**
   BORN 10-16-1905
   WHERE Winston Co., Miss.
   DIED
   WHERE

8. **Samuel L. Johnson**
   BORN 1-4-1850
   WHERE Monroe Co. (now Lee)
   WHEN MARRIED April 4, 1873
   DIED
   WHERE Mary and Jeffcoats

9. **Mary J. Fisher Jeffcoats**
   BORN 1879
   WHERE Ark.
   DIED
   WHERE

10. **Henry Harrison McBrew**
    BORN Nov. 30, 1841
    WHERE
    WHEN MARRIED Oct. 21, 1911 Oak Forrest
    WHERE Lee Co.

11. **Lou Vinnia Smith** 2nd wife
    BORN 3-26-1865
    WHERE
    DIED 11-23-1926
    WHERE

12. **George Washington Allen**
    BORN 1864
    WHERE Lee Co. Ark. 3rd wife of 3rd husband
    DIED 1927
    WHERE Willie Pulliam

13. **Willie Pulliam**
    BORN 1875 Meno (Lee Co.)
    WHERE
    DIED 1921
    WHERE Mariann

14. **Dyson Coy(e) Edwards**
    BORN 1880
    WHERE Oktibbeha Co., Miss.
    WHEN MARRIED
    DIED Jan. 1946
    WHERE San Jose Calif.
    Sadie Lee Parkes

15. **Sadie Eliza Parkes**
    BORN 7-11-1887
    WHERE Neshoba Co., Miss.
    DIED
    WHERE

16. Hardin Johnson 1812 Alabama
17. Elizabeth Day
18. William K Jeffcoat b. sc 1842
19. Nancy J. Fisher
20. John McBrew
21. Mary
22. A.B. Smith b. 1830   cant sure this Lois parents
23. E.A. Smith b. 1827
24. George W. Allen b. 1922 or 1839 Alabama
25.
26. William M. Pulliam b. 1852   m. 1879 march 12
27. Mary E. Clark b. 1852
28. Dr. William Edwards b. 1840 Alabama
29. Mary Jane Edwards Chochaw Miss. b. 9-4-1850
30. Asa Isaiah Parkes
31. Sudie Eliza Yates

Stephanie Johnson
Born 1947 (march 24)
Where Phillips Co. Ark.
Lived Marianna, Ark.
Lee Co.

married 1968 in
Lee Co. to
William P. Dixon
children Erin Elizabeth
May 30 1974
@ Scotia Paisley
April 19, 1979

The Peyton-Hill Family
"You'll All Need One Another"

To the rear of the Peyton house in Carlisle is an old cedar tree with broad, heavy branches that spread ten feet in all directions. Two of the lower branches are broken about a foot from the trunk. One is wrapped in styrofoam. The other, capped with a drinking glass, supports a worn harness ring, half-covered in leather. Two old, rusty door hinges, suspended from the same branch, hang about a foot below. To the left an iron spike juts out several inches from a natural flaw in the bark surface, while above a rectangular ceramic fuse-holder is firmly nailed against the trunk. Cascading from the upper branches is a wild assortment of rusty bedsprings and metal stripping. They fall, frozen by time and weather, around the other objects.

On first impression the arrangement seems an improvisation on the southern "bottle trees" that sport glass objects on branches in order to "catch" spirits that might disturb the harmony of a family house nearby (see "Bottle Trees," p. 52). "Junky" was the word one sophisticated family member used to describe the objects, but an astute observer can nevertheless make out some common features. All are products of technology; most have a clear domestic function; all surfaces, before rust dulled them, shone with "flash" brilliance: finally, all are physically integrated with the tree, seeming an extension, or at least a decoration of it. Having outlived their original functions, the objects gain from the tree a special status not shared by the useless discards in the storage shed a few paces away. Nobly elevated above the level of the human eye, they stand as reminders of home life in days gone by: the horse and buggy, the big front door, the electrical installation, the parents' big double bed.

What do these arborabilia mean? Today's family members are certain only that the flash is the handiwork of their father Charley Abraham Peyton, and that its kaleidoscopic brilliance are sparks from his private ideas. Since his death in the mid-Fifties, the tree has remained intact. Perhaps it is a statement about the family's transition from rural hardship to town comfort; the objects, like pictures in a photo album, might display a serial image of additions and improvements to the Peyton house. Or, perhaps, like the bottle trees, its purpose is actively protective, using household analogies to arrest evil and divert it from the house itself. Explanations about ideas Charley may have once attached to the assemblage have fallen away from family oral tradition. In its own language, however, the tree expresses one idea quite plainly: it stands in open celebration of past creation brought into permanent

Bottle Trees _____

Eudora Welty, in *The Wide Net and Other Stories* (New York: Harcourt, Brace, Jovanovich, 1971) supplied the following history of a bottle tree (p. 156): "Livvie knew that there could be a spell put in trees and she was familiar from the time she was born with the way bottle trees kept evil spirits from coming into the house — by luring them inside the colored bottles, where they cannot get out again. Solomon had made the bottle tree with his own hands over the nine years, in labor amounting to about a tree a year, and without a sign that he had any uneasiness in his heart, for he took as much pride in his precautions against spirits coming in the house as he took in the house, and sometimes in the sun the bottle trees looked prettier than the house did."

Robert Farris Thompson and Joseph Cornet have traced the influence of Kongo (Central African) belief and art on Afro-American cultural expressions. (In an exhibition catalog *The Four Moments of the Sun: Kongo Art in Two Worlds* (Washington: National Gallery of Art, 1981). One example is southern bottle trees. "There can be little doubt," they remark, "that the custom of guarding yards and households from all evil with branches decked with glass vessels came from Kongo and culturally-related territory in Central Africa" (p. 179). They trace the idea through the ports of New Orleans, Charleston, and the West Indies, to a tradition in which pottery vessels, as forerunners to glass, were attached to tree branches in family compounds and farms to protect the household and crops from evil.

L'Abée Proyart described this custom on the northern coast of the Kongo-speaking region *(Histoire de Loango, Kakongo, et autres royaumes d'Afrique* [Paris: Berton et Crepart, 1776, pp. 192-193): "All, after having cultivated their field, take care in order to drive away sterility and evil spells, to fix in the earth, in a certain manner, certain branches of certain trees, with some pieces of broken pots. They do more or less the same thing before their houses, when they must absent themselves during a considerable time. The most determined thief would not dare to cross their threshhold, when he sees it thus protected by these mysterious signs."

Professor William Wilsie Peyton attended Tuskeegee Institute before marrying the schoolteacher Eliza Hardin. She died shortly after the birth of her third child but inspired the Peyton women to work for the welfare of others.

conjunction with the tree's ongoing participation in the present. However sequestered old memories and ideas remain from modern minds, the tree itself bears witness to the hand of Charley Peyton, who created a life for his family and left a tree to remind them of it.

Self-Reliance. Those who know the ten brothers and sisters of the Peyton family say they display remarkable character: "creative," they observe, "independent," "responsible." Born in the ricelands of eastern Arkansas to the tree-maker Charley Peyton and his wife Princess Odell Green, the children divided their growing years between a home in Carlisle, where their father worked in the local rice mill, and their country farms nine miles north of town. These farms, owned by the Peyton and Green families for more than four generations, were a chief source of food. Each year the rich Peyton bottomland yielded a rice crop which, in an era of low rural incomes, was an important supplement to the family treasury. What Charley could not pay for in cash he acquired through intelligence and applied skill. He built their six-room town house to his own design, sided it with white asbestos, poured half-circle concrete steps that led to the front and back doors, dug a well, and built out-houses for storage. When he later added electricity, gas, and plumbing, the family recalls with pride that the city inspectors gave full approval to the finished work.

Charley was a model of self-reliance for his children, and each went

The pump at the Peyton home house in Carlisle reminds occupants of Charley Peyton, who built the house, wired it and plumbed it with his own hands.

on to excel as far as his abilities would allow. "Be independent," he would say. "Make your own job. Do something creative." Today Freddy Joe is a welder, Charles James a graduate of Baptist College and an employee at a rubber plant, William a graduate of Philander Smith College and a production manager at Remington, and Abraham a graduate of the Adult Education Center, auto mechanic and occasional songwriter. Of the sisters, Arcola is an upholsterer in Berkeley, California, Caroline an instructor at Hall High, Gloria Dean a special education teacher, Lorraine a teacher at Franklin School, and Laverta owner and manager of real estate. Shirley Peyton Hill, the sixth sister and family historian, recalls that her father balanced his emphasis on personal achievement with an equal insistence on their co-operation. "Togetherness was what my mother and father always taught," a point which Charley illustrated with a metaphor: "Now, if you're going to have quarrels, I want one to go to the West and one to go to the East and one to stay in the South and one to go in the North. That's if you're going to have differences. But it's not good that you do that. 'Cause you'll all NEED one another, every one!"

Whether in conscious loyalty to their father's charge or in response

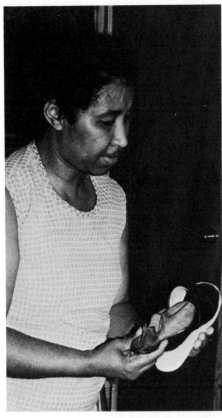

A sock-stretcher invented by Professor W. W. Peyton.

to a combination of forces that included his wish, the members of the Peyton family have always chosen to remain in close proximity. For a time, a sub-family composed of Laverta, Charles James, and Abraham was established in Boston, where Mother Odell's brother and three sisters lived. It was the Boston Peytons who welcomed their sister Shirley to a new start in life following her divorce from Edmund Hill. She looks back with amusement on her apprehension as she packed her four children, trunks, and footlockers on a Boston-bound train. From the little depot in Carlisle all the way to Memphis, her young ones watched the tears roll down her cheeks as they munched on cookies made as a farewell token by a former employer. "I'm going to a place I don't know," she reports thinking, "but I've made this step and I must go on." Peyton family closeness brought the journey to a happy conclusion. "When we got to Boston, everyone was bouncing and happy and my brothers and sister were there to meet me. And everything worked out well."

Family Rituals. Since the late Seventies, the family (with the exception of Arcola) has re-assembled in the Little Rock area, and the mutual welfare of its members is for each a day-to-day concern. Laverta's real estate acumen supplied Shirley with her downtown house;

Shirley's fondness for her nieces and nephews makes her a favorite baby-sitter among her sisters. Joint meals, telephone conversations, pop visits are routine throughout the week. Weekends are shared in trips to Petit Jean mountain, picnics to Burns Park, or barbecues in Shirley's backyard.

Times such as holidays, funerals, and birthdays, graduations, and Mother's Day give structured expression to the family's sense of solidarity. A strong equality typifies these events; each member contributes a proportioned share of food, labor, transportation, humor, and good will. The tradition goes back to childhood, where holidays such as Christmas were a collective responsibility. Odell Peyton encouraged her children to join in picking and shelling pecans, preparing the turkey and dressing and cranberry sauce, and in baking cakes and pies to suit their taste. On Christmas morning, toys were not the only proof of a visit by Santa Claus; he approved each child's dessert with the ultimate compliment: a missing slice. Today's contributions range over the entire meal in pot-luck fashion. Informal discussions over the telephone assign a dish to each brother or sister according to talent. "Meat," "dressing," "greens," "vegetables," "salads," "drinks," "breads" are categories designated and filled. "Sweets" is still an open category to which any member may contribute, although Gloria, the family's acknowledged dessert chef, is expected to provide at least one masterpiece.

The same spirit of co-operation dictates the setting for Christmas gatherings. Each year the gift-exchange on Christmas Eve and the early afternoon dinner the next day rotate among the Peyton households. Matter-of-fact gift talk always marks the start of the Peyton Christmas season. "What's on your mind for Christmas?" "Make it small." "Okay, give me five small things you want." On Christmas Eve night, after tunafish and cheese sandwiches, each Peyton loads his holiday wealth into a cardboard box brought for the purpose. Practical, household goods predominate: curtains, wine glasses, clocks, bathroom scales, a mug tree. All practical, except for the last gift. "Just when we're ready to go home, we line up these gag gifts on the table, just BEAUTIFULLY wrapped." Inside? "Maybe a bar of soap, an old shoe, a boot, an old pot, a crumpled-up newspaper. Last year [Shirley laughs] my brother wrapped up an old BONE!"

Only one Christmas custom is inconsistent with the general family rule of equal participation for all members. At the Peyton Christmas dinner, blessing is always the prerogative of the eldest adult male. Patriarchy is important in the family, as oral tradition plainly attests.

The Green's Secret Recipe For Barbecue Sauce _____
(Shirley: "You take tomato sauce, lemons, spices ... it's not a recipe to be given out to everybody. It came from my mother's side. She had three brothers who ran a barbecue stand in East St. Louis. They give it to one person in a generation. I have to give it to one of mine so she can pass it down.")

Family Ancestors. Any account of Peyton family history begins, as Shirley put it, with a son of "America's first people." Great-grandfather Tecumseh ("Tecumshin") Hardin was of Cherokee ancestry and a "high official in the tribe, maybe a chief." Recollections about his birthplace are dim. However, one family story records that India Ripley Payton, mother of Shirley's cousin Lois, received a letter from a Cherokee relative fifty years ago inviting her to visit his Oklahoma reservation; the family surmises that he must have left Oklahoma, then the "Indian Territory," sometime during or shortly after the Civil War.

In Arkansas, near Carlisle, Tecumseh acquired extensive land holdings, judging from the family inheritance. He married Ailie Nichols, who was herself part Indian. A hardworking woman, she gave birth to seventeen children and served as the community midwife. Ailie is credited with having encouraged her children to pursue an education that would be of service to others. Her daughter Eliza Hardin taught school throughout her short life, and her granddaughters chose to practice nursing. "It was handed down, Shirley observes, "a line of teachers, nurses, doctors. They always performed a duty and liked things that cultivated the mind."

Tecumseh marked the Peyton family with an enduring legacy of pride borne of self-reliance. "Indian people join together," Shirley says. "They grow their own food and just don't waste their time. Like them, we can do things to help ourselves and to help others." No one in the family better fulfilled this dictum that Eliza Hardin's husband William Wilsie ("Professor W. W.") Peyton. Of French and Indian ancestry, he and the family were led by their father Abraham from Virginia to Alabama, where "W. W." attended Tuskeegee Institute; then they moved to Arkansas, where his son completed his education at Baptist College. Family narratives make reference to the poems that grandfather Peyton presented to the Tuskeegee library; in later years he habitually left his verse strewn around the house or tucked away in a book or desk drawer. "W. W." was also a blacksmith and clever inventor. "He was very good at teaching and giving examples," says Shirley. One invention was a "sock-stretcher," a piece of metal cast in the shape of a foot. Its purpose was to stretch wool socks after washing into a wearable size. Another was a "skillet lifter." Shirley explained: "It was like a star-shaped thing with a handle. You put it right under the hot skillet or eye of the stove. It was very nice, and we wanted to keep it. My father kinda put it away, and it was something he treasured."

"W. W." was a respected schoolmaster in Carlisle, and older residents vividly recall his little one-room country schoolhouse, sparsely furnished with benches and a water barrel. It stood on the family farm until Professor Peyton moved his profession to a new location in town on the site of the Peyton homeplace. His wife Eliza taught through the birth of three children, but with the fourth her career ended in tragedy.

Returning too quickly to her duties after the child's delivery, she "became ill," say oral accounts, "with a female disorder" and died shortly after.

"Payton" was the original spelling of Professor Peyton's name. He spoke often to his children about his French ancestry, a claim not readily acknowledged by "Paytons" of a different racial background who lived in Carlisle. Moreover, in such a tiny community, mail to households having the same name was easily misdirected; "W. W." — "because of mail and other problems," as Shirley put it — was eventually pressed to relieve the confusion by changing his name. Thereafter, in the minds of some, the question of the mail was forever settled, along with the question of the Professor's personal ancestry.

Shirley never knew her grandfather but relates that he passed away mysteriously: "It was a peculiar thing. He kinda gave notice to them to watch the time on his last day of living. He said, "Now, when eleven o'clock gets here, y'all don't be afraid to tell me 'cause I'll be going away. So they looked. And the first time he asked, it was about ten o'clock; so he turned there and looked at the clock. And when it was close to eleven o'clock, he turned to ask again, and everybody refused to give him the time. But he went promptly at the time he said he was going to leave the world. It was amazing."

Among the seven children who survived Professor Peyton was Shirley's father, Charley Abraham. His wife, Odell Green, was a neighbor girl from a farm across the road. The families were linked by a longstanding friendship, and midwife Ailie Hardin assisted at baby Odell's birth. With the marriage, the family's Indian ancestry was again reinforced; for Odell's mother, Cora Powell Green, was descended from Indians "out of Mississippi."

Living Off The Land. Indian self-sufficiency, a legacy from both parents, is a recurrent theme in Shirley's reminiscences about childhood life in the country. Truck patches on the Green farm were planted in rows of Irish potatoes, sweet potatoes, corn, English peas, squash, onions

Cora Powell Green's Folk Beliefs
1. The Twelve Day Wash. Do not wash on the twelfth day after Christmas or else you'll wash away a member of the family.
2. Don't sweep another's feet. It runs the person away from home.
3. Hog jowl and black-eyed peas are "musts" on New Year's Day if you want to be happy or lucky the rest of the year.
4. On New Year's Day the first person to enter your home must be a man, and very dark. Otherwise "the year will turn around for you."
5. If you drop food, a fork, or a dish towel on the floor, a hungry guest will come soon. If you drop food from your mouth, someone is coming.
6. If a black cat crosses to the left in front of you, turn and go back. If it goes to the right, it's good luck.
7. Don't tell a dream before breakfast.

of all kinds, tomatoes, okra, cabbage, greens of various sorts, carrots, beets ... in short, every vegetable Shirley had ever desired or known. Milk cows provided butter, buttermilk, and cream. Turkeys, guineas, geese, ducks, and chickens (White Rock, Dominique, Leghorn, and Rhode Island Reds) gave eggs and meat. In summer and early autumn Cora made hominy in a big pot in the yard and canned vegetables and beef. In November, J. Henry butchered the hogs, salted them down, and smoked them for the winter.

Cora's ingenuity translated these harvests into fondly-remembered recipes for the family table. Nothing went to waste. Fried pork skin ("cracklin'") added to corn meal mix gave old-fashioned "cracklin' bread." Head cheese utilized the hog parts unsuited to smoking, as did sausage and pickled pig's feet. Onion tops could be fried and served as a side vegetable. Cabbages were soaked in brine for winter kraut. Favorite dishes were stewed tomatoes with bread, otherwise known as "tomato puddin'"; green tomatoes deep-fried in batter; a "sweet potato cobbler" that mixed the vegetable with bread, sugar, and butter; and hoe cakes, "a great big round concern" shaped from biscuit dough and quick-fried in the skillet, filling the house with a warm, comfortable smell. Pickled pears and watermelon rind pickle were winter fruits that complemented the walnuts and hickory nuts that children gathered on expeditions to the woods. Indeed, the production and enjoyment of food was so central to the family's life together that much of the memorabilia handed down from older relatives includes items they once used in the kitchen. An old pressure cooker, a food mill, a butter churn, a milk pitcher, are tangible reminders of their agricultural past.

Cora Green was convinced that, just as food nourished, many of nature's products possessed an innate healing power. "At times," Shirley recalls, "when we would say, 'Oh, we have a headache today, grandmother,'" she would go out to the peach tree, get peach leaves, and bind them to our heads with a tight band." A sharpened twig from a sweet gum tree was a medicinal toothpick. Sassafras tea was a year-round tonic, while poke sallet greens, taken twice a year, purified the body "like mineral oil."

Following grandmother Green's example, the Peyton girls learned how to use old dresses as patterns for new ones and to re-use old cloth by making aprons or quilts. "Boy" quilts were a patchwork of old blue jeans or khaki pants stuffed and then stitched. The training ground for boys was the rice farm, which Charley created and constantly improved. To ensure that plenty of water would be available at all times, he dug a twelve-foot concrete canal that distributed the water through steel pipes into an irrigation system of small channels and ditches.

A Family Tragedy. The irrigation system was a blessing and a curse. Sister Deborah drowned in its waters at the age of eighteen. Her picture is prominently displayed among the family photographs, often

Sister Dorothy Peyton shortly before her tragic drowning death in an irrigation canal on the family rice farm.

jointly with a snapshot of the canal where she died. Deborah's death was a double blow to the family. Not only was she deeply loved, but she personified many of the best features of family talent. Shirley recalls: "Deborah was a very cheerful girl. She was very artistic and had many skills. She could make dresses without a pattern. And her marks in school were straight A's. She did a lot of interior decorating in the home and other things. She carried on the skilled tradition that my grandfather created during his time."

Deborah's death has been enshrined in a story often repeated among the family members, and its retelling unites their emotions in a common understanding of the family values for which she stood. Over time the incident has been kept alive in dramatic re-enactment by different tellers, who in this way take stock of their own roles in the unfolding of events. Shirley's account is recorded in two versions. Here is one of them: "At the time that that happened, I was at the town house. My daddy's sister and daughter were there. They wanted to go out to the farm and kind of look around. I was getting ready to prepare a dinner: chicken, potato salad, greens, cornbread...a great big country dinner in town. So, one of the cousins wanted to stay with me ... her name was Dorothy. My sister and brother were out there on the farm. So, on the way out there, my aunt, my mother, and another cousin, were approaching their way up to the knell. My father called to their attention the place where my sister had come up and sunk back down for the third time and then sunk into something like quicksand on the bottom. When they got there, she had come up for the third time, and they were all trying to save her. Now my brother Abraham, he went off into the water. She took hold of him, but because he was younger, he shook her loose. They called for my father. He was off irrigating rice and had to come from a distance; he had his boots on; he tried to jump into the water, but got caught in the quicksand. She was eighteen years old and five feet tall in a twelve-foot pond."

Dreams And Visions. Like her mother and grandmother, Shirley is endowed with the power of prediction through dreams, a power which she calls an "Indian gift." These experiences are not invention; rather, they are a burden which not all family members readily accept. In general, the men take them less seriously than the women. Shirley believes that one receives the gift through grace and activates it through free will: "Some chosen people who want dreams will get them."

Shirley begins her second version of the story about Deborah's death (see "The Predicting Power of Visions and Dreams," below) with such a dream. It disturbed her sleep on the eve of the accident, and with hindsight she is convinced it contained an implicit warning about the

The Predicting Power of Visions and Dreams————————————————

(Among Peyton women, the power to predict the future through visions and dreams is an inherited endowment, an "Indian gift." It is a serious burden, one accepted with mixed feelings. These stories are not invention. They are accounts of genuine human experience meant to instruct later generations in how to interpret experiences of a similar kind.)

• Shirley's dream in Boston.

I dream a lot of true dreams. I told my daughter Kay, "I dreamed I saw you in bed in the back room and someone, a real dark fellow, was reaching his arm in at the glass door, in your back door. He was coming in, breaking in last night. You were hollering, 'Mama!' A way back sound."

She said, "Oh no, Mama. The people downstairs — somebody broke in THEIR apartment."

I said, "Yes, but this was YOUR apartment." It was on Elton Street.

She said, "No, no," as if to say, "That can't happen to me."

That Saturday night she called. They went someplace and came back. "Mama, your dream is TRUE." When they came in the back door was open and the window was broken. They came in just like I saw it.

• Shirley's dream the night before Deborah drowned.

I have different dreams. The night before my sister Deborah drowned I saw a yellow and white car jumping in dry space, in nothing but dry land. My mother came to the bedroom. She said, "Shirley?" I said, "What?" She said, "Can't you sleep?" I said, "No, I can't sleep tonight." She said, "Come into my room." I said, "Naw, I'll sleep here in the girl's room." (You know, there was the girl's room, the boy's room, and my mother and father's room.)

So, the next morning she got up and she said, "Now you can tell your dream after breakfast." I said [in a high, strong voice] "A yellow and white car was just doing that way in that new ground, that newly-dug dirt." She said, "Hmmm." "I didn't see anybody in the car. The car was just going by itself, just going."

So, at about 10:00 my daddy said, "Who wants to go to the farm?" And Mama said, "YOU SHOULDN'T let those children go out there — those are GIRLS. You shouldn't want them to go." Deborah said, "I wanna go, Daddy." I said, "I don't like that. You can't see anything but woods ... "

So about 10:30 that morning my Aunt Dixie and her daughter Dorothy came down. And so my mother, some way, wanted to go out to the farm with them. I said, "I'll stay home and cook dinner." I had four chickens made, you know, gettin' them ready. About that time I looked out the back door into the driveway and they were drivin' in and my mother was yellin' to the top of her voice. She said [in a high falsetto], "Shirley," said, "Deborah's drowned at hooommme!" She was hollering. At that time we didn't have a telephone. I ran up to the little town which was about five blocks away from where my home was. I went up to the store and these white people there, Mrs. Cooke, she said, "What's wrong, Peyton? What's wrong?" So they sent the firemen out there, but she'd been gone about twenty minutes. That was the time of our life.

Now that was the dream, if she had taken on to it. But my father didn't want to listen.

This sister that drowned came back one night. I guess it was the same way I would say a dream. Placed her left hand all the way around the table. She had made a striped shirt and she was wearing it, with a pocket on the side and a white blouse. And when she went all the way around the table, she stood in front of the girls' room. And I said, "Ahhh ... look. YOU SHOULDN'T have gone. Mama said, 'Don't,' and you just wanted to." She said, "Yes, I wanted to. After the things you said, I shouldn't have, huh?" I said, "Nooo! You're not havin' NO fun!" She said, "That's all YOU know."

And when she got ready to go, she asked me to go with her. And when she took me away, she took me away in the high loft — like a gym or something — way in the attic, way up. And all I could see was like flares and tissue paper, just little bitty things, just a cluster of little things.

It goes on now. My children have dreams and all.

• Shirley's mother, Odell Green Peyton, dreams about her husband's accident.

My mother told my father a voice came to her three times and said, "Tell Charley, don't go to work today. He's going to get seriously injured." Mama got up. She couldn't sleep that night. She said, "Charley, don't go to work today because a voice came to me last night." He said, "You just don't tell me that." (You know, a lotta times people don't believe and don't want those kinds of things told to them.) "No, you just don't tell me that. I have to go to work. I got a big family here."

"A voice came three times."

"I'm going to work."

Mama made his breakfast. He went to work at the rice mill. At twelve o'clock he came home. Mama had lemon pie, just a beautiful dinner. He sat down and ate. "What was that you said this morning about that dream? Nothing has happened yet." He kinda laughed.

They brought him home on a stretcher at two o'clock. A boy had asked him for a Coke, and when he said, "You know where the machine is," the boy said, "You old so and so, you got a smart word." He took a Coke bottle, popped my daddy's head and laid it in.

presence of harmful forces in the dry ground of the family farm. On hearing the dream, her mother understood its significance and tried indirectly to dissuade her daughters from visiting the farm the next day.

The grief of Deborah's death is partly relieved in Shirley's next account, telling of a vision in which the girl returns and invites her sister to follow her to heaven. Shirley remembers rising "way up, like in an attic," an image that recalls the reports of near-death experiences in the seriously ill. Whether or not her "sympathetic death" is a genuine product of psychic power, Shirley's belief in her gift is reinforced by legends of such powers in other family members; for example: "Mother would tell things that would happen, and they would come true. She told one of her cousins, 'You're goin' away with your husband overseas. You'll be back in ONE MONTH. You'll stay with him one month.' She turned around and told the girl's sister, she said, 'You, you're going to marry someone who's crippled.' Later they both said, 'Odell, what you said is so true!'"

Like her mother, Shirley forecasts events only for kin. Whatever its origin, the "gift" must be practiced without doing injury to the privacy of strangers. "Would YOU like to have forewarnings about different things?" she asked directly. Her matter-of-fact answer: "Yes and no."
                                                        —Lois Pattillo
                                                        Deirdre LaPin

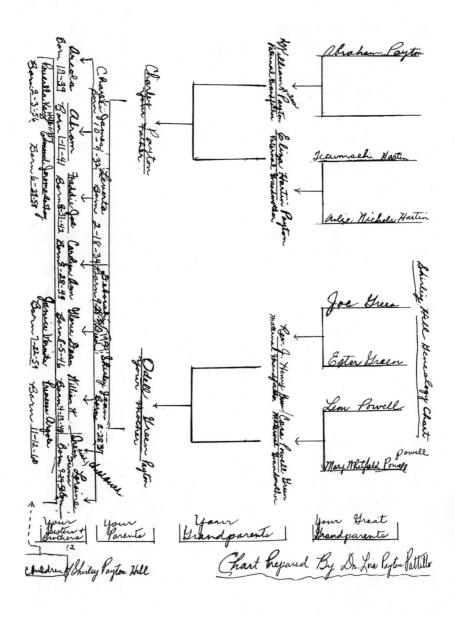

Shirley Hill Genealogy Chart

Abraham Payton

William and Eliza Martin Payton
Paternal Grandparents

Tecumseh Martin

Alie Nichols Martin

Charley Payton
Paternal Father

Charles James
Born 10-9-32

Leneta
Born 2-18-34

Alola
Born 1-9-39

Abram
Born 1-11-41

Freddie Joe
Born 8-31-42

Carolyn Ann
Born 3-28-44

Gloria Dean
Born 6-5-46

William H.
Born 4-13-48

Gwendolyn
Born 7-22-59

Ardis Loraine
Born 9-4-96

Ramona Angela
Born 11-12-60

Russell Kimberly Emanuel Jerome Anthony
Born 6-21-59

Russell Kimberly
Born 3-3-56

Joe Green

Ester Green

Lem Powell

Mary Whitfield Powell
Powell

Rev. J. Henry Powell Cora Powell Green
Maternal Grandfather Maternal Grandmother

Odell Green Payton
Your Mother

Your Sisters & Brothers | Your Parents | Your Grandparents | Your Great Grandparents

12

Children of Shirley Payton Hill

Chart Prepared By Dr. Lois Payton Pattillo

Ferdinand Kanis and Family in about 1890. To his left clockwise are
Emelia Louise, his wife Margarethe Wilhelmina Thoma, John Ferdinand,
Katherine Margarethe ("Minnie"), and Edward.

The Keller-Henry Family
A German Pioneer Legacy

On a summer day in 1878, Ferdinand Kanis, grandfather of Marguerite Henry, boarded a train in Pittsburgh with his wife, two children, and their few possessions. He was joining, at the age of twenty-six, a new wave of German immigrants seeking cheap land across the Mississippi River in the state of Arkansas. Six years of labor in Pittsburgh's steel mills had seasoned the young man to life in America. It equipped him with a knowledge of English, a grasp of Yankee customs, U.S. citizenship papers, and $37, barely enough capital to see him through the costs of resettlement. As the train made its way through the hills of western Pennsylvania, Ohio, and across the prairies of Indiana toward St. Louis, it carried this young son of a Saxon farmer deeper into the new country he had chosen for his home.

But Ferdinand Kanis had not, nor would he ever, shed the unmistakable stamp of the Fatherland that bore him. To his family and many of his friends, he was in spirit a German: a man of hearty humor, direct opinions, compassion, and a zeal for discipline and hard work. While his preferences in food, houses, language, and music could be counted among external expressions of his Saxon soul, it was his German spirit, more than any tangible earmarks of culture, that helped shape the lives of the family who survived him. It underlay a traditional "pattern for living" that guides the family still; Marguerite summed up the "pattern" this way: "If a job needs doing — it doesn't matter WHAT the job is — and there is nobody to do it, you learn HOW to do it, and you do it

BEST."

Like the nearly four thousand Germans who had come to Arkansas before him, Ferdinand Kanis faced what was indeed an ambitious task. From the Gateway City, the St. Louis, Iron Mountain, and Southern Railway would steam through Missouri to northeast Arkansas and then cut diagonally across the state to Altus, the nearest terminus to Little Rock. On disembarkation, the young man in search of farmland would be pressed to make a choice. For, by 1872, there were eight million acres of state lands available with 1,700,000 acres in the Little Rock district alone. Prices were low: fifty cents an acre for swampland and $1.25 for "internal development lands," whose revenue was to be used by the state for building canals and railroads. Railroad land grants, though slightly dearer, held an even greater attraction for the immigrant. When the major rail lines were completed in 1876, the companies opened an active campaign to lure prospective settlers. Railroads could offer a newcomer land with the added attractions of a free train ticket to Arkansas, long financing, secure titles, and ready access to transportation.

History In Family Folklore. Although it was a railroad advertisement for Delta bottomland that attracted Ferdinand to Arkansas at the outset, family oral tradition tells how he came to make the classic pioneer choice and became instead a homesteader. As Marguerite tells the story (See "Ferdinand Kanis Homesteads Near Little Rock," below), his motive was not economic, though his 160 acres of homestead cost only a small title fee. What induced him to abandon his dream of buying cottonland was the concrete prospect of starting out life with Joe

Ferdinand Kanis Homesteads Near Little Rock _____

My grandfather, Ferdinand Kanis, worked in Pittsburgh in a steel mill and said, "That is not for me," because he had grown up on a farm in what at that time was Thuringen — Thuringia — and had, as many young men, the desire to better himself. AND he did NOT want to be in the army; you see, that was the period of the Franco-Prussian War [1870-1871].

So, after working in Pittsburgh for awhile, he said, "I'm going to spend my life doing this. I'm going to hunt something better." And he had in his mind to come to Pine Bluff, Arkansas, and buy cottonland. On the way down from St. Louis he met another German, and this German was going to stop at Little Rock. And so, he persuaded my grandfather to get off the train at Little Rock and they would go see about some farmland. Which they did. Homesteaded. And stayed just west of town.

They both settled west of town, which is HILLY. They didn't settle on farmland AT ALL. It meant that all the farming they did had to be helped. But not too long thereafter they both started dairies and had fine dairies. What they did then was to grow everything; they grew wheat, they grew oats, they grew rye, they grew hay for the cattle, they grew a GREAT kitchen garden — better than a kitchen garden, really, because it had rows and rows of corn. Then they had goats, sheep, hogs, and chickens. Except for sugar, salt, and a few other items, it was self-sustaining.

Ties with the old country. A postcard in German script shows a barn rebuilt after a fire on the Kanis farm in Saxony.

Hirscheider, a German friend. From the characterization that runs through Marguerite's recollections of him, Ferdinand Kanis emerges as a man who cared deeply about people. Describing him in later years she observes, "My mother said he was a wonderful father, and my father said he was the best friend he ever had in his life."

Marguerite's story, overall, is harnessed to a more far-reaching purpose. It is a migration story; it explains to the family the reasons for their ancestor's decision to leave his home in Teichwolframsdorf, Saxony, and face the challenge of life in an unknown land. Leaving the Pittsburgh steel factory with the words "THAT is NOT for ME," he voices the attitude his descendants claim he left them as a legacy: to accept only "the best" in their lives. "I'm not going to spend my life doing this," he says again, "I'm going to hunt something better." Marguerite's story reconstructs history in order to single out this motive, interpret it in light of a present-day value, and make it the central focus of the tale.

What begins as a historical migration story, then, becomes a family parable. Ferdinand Kanis, the American pioneer hero, is at the same time an exemplar of a family maxim. His intention to "better himself" at the start of his journey sets off a chain of events that lead to his success. Here, the specific experiences of Ferdinand Kanis prove the general family truth that success is possible when it is buttressed by confidence, determination, and hard work. In this way the history of an ancestor is made to do double duty by suggesting that the past be taken as a model for the present. Ferdinand succeeded in fulfilling his aspirations, and today his descendants may, by his example, be inspired to do so again.

In a more comical vein the family tells a companion story about the pragmatic Mrs. Kanis, who was openly skeptical about Ferdinand's plans to start a new life in Arkansas. Katherine Margarethe Wilhelmine Thoma was an independent young woman from the village of Festenbergsgrauth, Bavaria. At eighteen she secured a post as a domestic worker for a family living in Winona, Minnesota, and crossed the Atlantic before joining her family (parents, one sister, and six brothers), who settled in East Liberty, Pittsburgh's German community. The Thomas were an active group (one, Marguerite recalls, owned a saloon in the neighborhood), and their burgher prosperity probably contrasted with the modest income of the factory worker Kanis, who lived in a boardinghouse nearby. Within two years of coming to the city, Wilhelmine and Ferdinand were married.

Understandably, Wilhelmine's attachment to Pittsburgh was better grounded than her husband's, and it was with considerable reluctance that she readied herself and her two babies, John Ferdinand (two years) and Wilhelmine Katherine Margarethe ("Minnie," Marguerite's mother, then six months), for the long journey west. Marguerite recalls the anecdote as told by her grandmother: "My grandmother said that she could not see coming to a place like this. And her parents said, 'Go TRY it.' And because it was so rough and unpromising, she did not unpack her trunk for a year (laughter). Because she KNEW (now laughing heartily) she could get money to get back to Pittsburgh! But by that time my grandfather had kind of worked things out, and so they got along very well."

Places And Things. The rich legacy of material achievement inherited from the life that Ferdinand Kanis "worked out" is especially noteworthy given its rudimentary beginnings. His granddaughter Edwina Atkinson, who today lives on the old Kanis farm, strives to imagine behind the vast spread of outbuildings, orchards, and cleared fields the one-room log house that young Kanis built with tools and a pair of mules bought with his modest funds. He added to his treasury of livestock by selling timber from clearing land, while his wife traded or exchanged products in excess of the family's needs — eggs, meat, feed, vegetables, leather — with other, often German, settlers. By the time his two youngest children Edward and Emelia were grown, the farm had a "big barn" for the dairy cattle and several little barns for sheep and goats, workhorses and mules. Later on there were well houses, a chicken house, a sweet potato house, an Irish potato house, a smokehouse, and a pumphouse driven by a windmill; a carriage shed, binder shed, and more sheds added later for modern farm machinery; pens for geese, guineas, and hogs; a cellar for cider and vinegar, another for wine made from cultivated grapes and wild varieties such as muscadines and scupper-

The Kanis farm west of Little Rock.

nongs, and a third cellar for fruits and vegetables; a grist mill, a smithy, and a sawmill. A German-designed cattle-feeder was the most intriguing structure. Called the "haystack" by the family, the two-story frame kept hay reserved in the upper level from which it was dropped or pulled by bovine mouths into an open area beneath protected by a wide overhang. The haystack's immense girth allowed twenty cows or more to feed at one time. Livestock also fed on the farm's rye, wheat, corn, and oats. Kanis gardens, orchards, slaughterhouse, and beehives supplied food to local grocers until the Second World War, and for several decades the sawmill produced lumber that helped build the growing towns of Little Rock and its northern neighbor.

Though damaged by a tornado in the mid-sixties, much of the old Kanis farm still stands. In 1932 the main house was moved closer to the front road with jacks and rolling logs, as Ferdinand's son Edward Kanis feared the wood shingles of the surrounding buildings might catch fire in the great Dust Bowl drought. Except for the kitchen garden, the orchards and fields no longer produce, but they are nevertheless a fertile ground for memories.

Upon this landscape, Marguerite's recollections impose another one peopled with faces from the past. An infinite variety of keepsakes is the catalyst for reviving images of this other time. They bear witness to the strict regularity of everyday rituals in the Kanis "pattern for living." "There was," Marguerite put it, "so much to do." The men on the dairy farm rose to milk at three o'clock, separated the cream, poured the fresh liquid into vats, and then loaded it onto the milk wagon that Mrs. Kanis would drive to town at dawn. The family still keeps the dippers that measured the milk into pitchers and bowls held by patient hands waiting along the road. Meanwhile, as the cattle ranged, other hands set to work tilling, mowing, bread-baking (at least every Saturday), washing, canning, sausage-making, corn-shucking (on rainy days), or preparing one of the sizeable meals served as a matter of custom to the family, laborers, and neighbors come on pleasure or on business. A few pieces from the old Kanis kitchen have made their way into the Henry household as part of the cooking tools women habitually pass on to their daughters. They include a copper kettle for making preserves (which Mrs. Henry's son now uses as a wastebasket) and several ever-functional iron skillets.

Other keepsakes speak of the mutual support family members showed one another in the course of their daily routine. One Marguerite mentioned was a quarter: "My mother said when they were growing up they always had hard washings, with overalls and all of these things; and, they obviously did their own washing and ironing. And she said if there was a pair of extra dirty overalls, she and my aunt KNEW there would be something in the pocket. So there would be a quarter in the pocket!"

Three o'clock was round-up time on the old Kanis farm, and the evenings were reserved for music, crafting, and games. Marguerite remembers her grandparents were "fantastic" at games of mental arithmetic. The boys, John and Edward, practiced tunes on the mandolin and guitar, as they were often asked to play at Saturday-night dances. Ferdinand carved furniture and tools, including a rolling pin and two tables preserved by the modern Henrys; Marguerite has also kept the cards Wilhelmina used to clean wool.

Other rituals which family memory attached to the old farm were more occasional in character: Ferdinand's monthly business trips to town, children's Sunday baseball games and ice cream fests, weekend visits by brothers and sisters from school in town, and — later — summer-long visits from grandchildren town-bound during the rest of the year. A treasure of handmade lace, linens, bedspreads, and clothing bears witness to generations of slow evenings and afternoons when women traded stories and news over needlework traditions brought from their German homeland. In rooms throughout the Henry home, these crafts give concrete expression to Marguerite's feeling of continuity with these traditions. Her children also know that feeling. Eldest daughter Elsa, for example, needing a party dress, will dip into boxes of tissue-wrapped blouses and skirts saved from her grandmothers and aunts. She takes secret pleasure in knowing that she has, for a fleeting moment, recharged them with life.

A Community Of Germans. In pursuing its German life-style, the Kanis family was not alone. Little Rock had attracted many German-speaking immigrants, and they soon jelled into a solid, hardworking community dedicated to town development. It was natural that the closest bonds grew between those families sharing a common faith

A wealth of handmade German lace. (Below) A bedspread crocheted long ago by Keller hands is put to use in the Henry household.

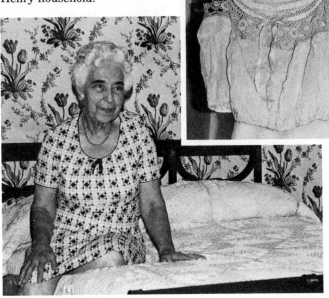

(Catholics, Protestants, Jews) or a common regional background (Austrian, Swiss, Bavarian, Bohemian), but they intermingled easily in commerce, politics, sports, entertainment, and the celebration of German holidays. These activities did not necessarily exclude other Americans, who shopped at German bakeries and stores, or attended dances and sporting events at the local Turnverein. Indeed, Germans were visible leaders in the larger community. Ferdinand Kanis, and later his sons, became commissioners charged with hiring labor and supervising the construction of roads. Brady School, which served children west of town, was built on a site by Father Kanis with a thousand dollars from his own treasury. If Germans were pillars of the community in their public lives, however, most expected their private needs to be met by their own group. Language, religion, schooling, friendship, and marriage were institutions generally monitored and maintained with other Germans. Until the outbreak of World War I, external pressure to conform to Anglo-American culture was slight. Kanis children — girls and boys — attended German-language school at the First Lutheran

Neighbors enjoy a Grütliverein or "land-clearing party" in the Kanis neighborhood.

Church downtown. The Kanis' worshipped at a smaller west-side Lutheran church on Eleventh and Ringo that housed a German congregation. Sunday picnics, birthday celebrations, and musical evenings took place in the company of German friends. Collective landclearing parties called *grütliverein* attracted Germans and Swiss to neighboring farms, where the chopping and stumping was rewarded with plenty of beer, ice cream, music, and joyous indulgence (see photo, above). Of the Kanis children who married, all chose German spouses: John wed Emma Rubach; Edward wed Edwina Taubman; and "Minnie," Marguerite's mother, wed a newcomer to America, Max Frederick Wilhelm Keller.

Grimma, a small town in the region of Lausitz near Leipzig, was Max Keller's home. Family tradition records that the Kellers descended from a line of royal attendants called *Marschall*, who were expert in the care of noblemen's horses. Max's grandfather Karl Johann and his father Karl Wilhelm both inherited the post, and it is likely that only immigration prevented Max from following suit. He was living with his grandfather (his mother died at his birth) in 1882 when his father, his father's new wife, and daughter Fanny joined a group of thirty-four families traveling to Benton, Arkansas. Karl's brother Otto and his sister Helen Wildt were also in the party. In 1895 their sister Selma made the journey and took employment as a professional cook in Little Rock for the Watkins on Scott Street. It was her Sherman Street home that welcomed Max Keller when he arrived, a mere lad, at the age of fourteen.

Wilhelmine Kanis, his future mother-in-law, would later vow to her children that "she had never seen such a rosy-cheeked little boy" as the Max Keller who collected milk from the Kanis dairy wagon. "People just

(Left) "Minnie" marries the
Saxon-born Max Keller.
(Above) Little Marguerite
Keller.

loved him," Marguerite declares, and he readily found odd jobs in
downtown shops while going to school at night to learn the English
language. Soon he struck out for California, where he worked in an
import-export establishment, writing "Minnie" faithfully during his
four-year absence. After their wedding in 1906, he planned to return to
the West, but "Minnie" was firmly rooted. Ferdinand Kanis gave them a
lot on the corner of Twelfth and Lewis, on the "edge" of town. Here, at the
end of the streetcar line, they opened a general mercantile store with
living quarters upstairs.

Their daughter Marguerite and her younger brother Carl grew up
in what she calls the best of two worlds. Their generation, grounded in
many of the old ways, became a watershed in the transition from a
German to an American way of life. Marguerite saw great contrasts
between her grandmother's old country social circle, the diverse clien-
tele in the Keller store, and the conformity of public school. "I thought it
was great," she says of straddling cultural domains. "I could do anything
I liked." Well, not everything. One significant exception was a clear
attack on her German name. "Margarethe" (or, a variant, "Margarete")
had been passed on in the family since the time of the great-
grandmother Margarethe Barbara Berlein. On her first day at Robert E.
Lee School, her "very well-known and very well-liked" teacher Bessie
Evans asked each child his name. "And I said 'Mar-ga-REET' because
that was the English way of pronouncing M-A-R-G-A-R-E-T-E. And so

she wrote it down, and apparently the French spelling was what she grew up with. And forever, that was it!" The German tradition was re-established with the birth of Marguerite's granddaughter Margarete, bearer of a very old naming tradition indeed.

Cuisine. As a general rule, national groups first lose their hold on language and last their taste for distinctive cuisine. An orthographic shift in a family name would be more easily digested than substitutes for *Klösse* (potato dumplings), sauerkraut and pork, Sauerbraten, Wiener Schnitzel, or fresh cottage cheese with onion and caraway seed. These were the dishes that appeared at Sunday dinner, the chief family ritual for the Kanis-Keller group. Add *Handkäse* (a Limburger-like cheese), *Strudel*, homemade sausage, sweet and sour cabbage, and a "big and wide" noodle dish (made with peppers, onions, cheese, and fresh tomatoes), and a wide variety of meals became possible. If the meal was cooked on the farm, an old rooster might be served, or — as a variation — a kid baked in the big iron range.

Family feasting reached its apogee in the yearly reunion "Tante" (Aunt) Selma called to honor her birthday. Many dishes were the same, but she infused them with her professional magic. Scores of relatives would collect around her modest house, eating in shifts and exchanging news. It was fitting that this elegant and independent woman should

Survivals: German Sayings From The Kanis Family

(Marguerite Henry remembers these sayings from childhood as expressions of family philosophy. Her mother inherited them from her father, Ferdinand Kanis. "I quote them in translation to my children.")

Man proposes, the Lord disposes.	Man denkt, Gott lenkt.
Take the broom along (if afraid of the dark).	Nimm' den Besen mit.
The Lord knows why he doesn't let the goat's tail grow longer: he'd knock his eyes out.	Der liebe Gott weisz warum Er den Geisenschwantz hat nicht länger wachsen lassen: sonst schlägt er sich die Augen aus.
I didn't fall on my mouth. (I always speak up.)	Bin nicht auf den Mund gefallen.
Sweep it under the rug.	Unter den Teppich Kehren.
What one doesn't have in his head. he has in his feet. (Making extra trips for something you forget.)	Was man nicht im Kopf hat, hat er in den Füszen.
Consider the source!	Bendenke den Ursprung!

preside over the annual gathering of the Keller clan; for, she herself was an institutional bulwark against family misfortune. She is most remembered for her prompt decision to assume responsibility for her niece Fanny's three young children after they were orphaned by two closely timed disasters: first, the accidental shooting death of Fanny's husband who was the mistaken target of a hired gunman and second, Fanny's own death from cancer.

A Woman's Place. Marguerite remembers "Tante" Selma as the embodiment of the family's most cherished traits. Concern for others, a striving for perfection, industry, and independence are recurrent motifs in Kanis and Keller family lore. These characterize the family's women as much as its men. Though a husband and wife divided their labor, the work of each was valued equally; they were partners in the common enterprise of raising a family and making it economically secure. Decision-making was always a two-way affair. Marguerite recalls that "neither one did anything without consulting the other. They were together on everything." To underscore the point, the family tells a cautionary anecdote about the time Ferdinand Kanis went ahead with a business deal against his wife's advice. "He was very eager about this... just because the man was German. But this German was a CROOK, and really it caused great problems."

A corollary to the notion of equal partnership was the family's commitment to the education of women. Marguerite describes both of her grandparents as "educated people;" her uncle Edward Kanis would often lament the wasted talent of a neighbor's uneducated daughters; tradition holds that Max Keller's grandmother marked him for a professorship, but unfortunately she died when he was fourteen, and he left for America. It was Marguerite who realized his missed opportunity by taking to heart her father's words, "In America, a woman can do anything she wants and is qualified to do." What Marguerite wanted was to perfect her knowledge of a family legacy, the German language. She crowned her bachelor's degree from the University of Arkansas with graduate studies at Indiana University and the University of Wisconsin. While serving as a teaching fellow in Indiana's Department of German, she was appointed Dean of Women and remained in the post until her marriage. Both of her daughters have professional training: Elsa is a registered medical record administrator, Katherine a dietary consultant for hospitals and nursing homes. Son Reid is a physician.

Marguerite's German heritage joined forces with a strong English tradition when she married Charles Reid Henry, a North Little Rock obstetrician descended from a British grandmother. With hindsight Marguerite laughingly suggests that the union was pre-ordained; after the marriage she learned that "his father was my mother's favorite dance partner."

Holidays. Clearest evidence of the entwined Keller-Henry traditions can be found in the celebration of family holidays. "We always made much of Christmas," says Marguerite, looking back on her childhood. As the season approached, Ferdinand Kanis would select a tree from his own woodlands and adorn it with German glass ornaments and candles. It was always a shimmering surprise to the Keller children, who were not allowed to see it until Christmas morning. Candles were lit only once during the season; they were dangerous in the house of all-wood construction.

Dinner was arranged by the Keller household. Aunt Emelia, a "second mother" to Marguerite and Carl, would purchase wholesale quantities of nuts and glacé fruit for making *Stollen* (a coffee cake), *Strudel*, American fruitcake, meringue cookies with nuts, and a variety of small cakes; the more complicated *pfeffernüssle* cookies were ordered from the bakery.

On the nearest Sunday to Christmas (the Keller store was always open on other days), the Kanis grandparents would arrive at the Keller home for a meal of *Klösse* goose, sauerkraut, noodles, vegetables, and cucumber salad with vinegar. After the Henrys were married, the German tradition was shifted to Christmas eve, when the young family was invited to the Keller's for a dish of pork, sauerkraut, *Klösse*, and cranberries.

The Henry parents, on the other hand, were very English. Christmas dinner for them meant turkey with sausage balls, quail, celery and other vegetables, and the obligatory Christmas suet pudding. Biscuits were an American addition. The rich pudding with rum sauce remained on the menu after the Henry couple began Christmas dinners at their own home, and the Henry women would collect in Marguerite's kitchen to perform joint labor over suet, carrots, fruits, nutmeats, all carefully steamed and wrapped. Pies are a lighter substitute today and the quail and biscuits have been shifted to Christmas breakfast. A special addition to their dinner is Dr. Henry's favorite dish from boyhood, an Italian turkey giblet casserole with "mostaccioli," fancy macaroni noodles.

Italian pasta, Christmas pudding, sweet and sour cabbage: today's Christmas dinner is a culinary metaphor for the great American melting pot. Its message is that traditions are not "lost;" rather, they are amalgamated by families into cultural expressions befitting a new context. In Marguerite's experience, this evolution has been so natural that she puzzles about the nation's recent emphasis on ethnicity. "People today are concerned about where they came from or carrying something over," she remarks. "The Germans were constantly hammering on the idea of being American. When my grandfather Kanis was criticised for being German in World War I, he went out and sold more liberty bonds than anyone else in Pulaski County. He said, 'Why do you think I left Germany if I didn't want to be an American?'" Today the citizens of Little Rock view Ferdinand Kanis as a founding father, and the family name honors its roads and parks. As his descendants continue in that inexorable fusion of origins that is the hallmark of American life, they remain aware of one thread in that cultural tapestry: Ferdinand Kanis and his German spirit, a legacy for a family, and by extension, a town.

—Deirdre LaPin

Commonwealth of Pennsylvania,
ALLEGHENY COUNTY.

Be it Remembered, That at a **COURT OF COMMON PLEAS, No. 1** held at the City of Pittsburgh, in and for the County of Allegheny, in the Commonwealth of Pennsylvania, in the United States of America, on the 23rd day of May in the year of our Lord, one thousand, eight hundred and seventy eight Ferdinand Kanis

a native of Germany exhibited a petition, to be admitted to become a Citizen of the United States. And it appearing to the satisfaction of the Court, that he had resided within the limits and under the jurisdiction of the United States for five years immediately preceeding his application, and that during that time he had behaved as a man of good moral character, attached to the principles of the Constitution of the United States, and well disposed to the good order and happiness of the same, and that he had in all things fully complied with the laws of the United States, in such case made and provided: and having declared on his solemn oath before the said Court, that he would support the **CONSTITUTION OF THE UNITED STATES**, and that he did absolutely and entirely renounce and abjure all allegiance and fidelity to every foreign prince, potentate, state or sovereignty whatever, and particularly to the Duke of Saxon Ferdinand Kanis of whom he was heretofore a subject: whereupon the Court admitted the said Ferdinand Kanis to become a **CITIZEN OF THE UNITED STATES**, and order all proceedings to be recorded by the Prothonotary of said Court, which was done accordingly.

In Testimony Whereof I have hereunto set my hand and affixed the seal of the said Court at the City of Pittsburgh, this 23rd day of May Anno Domini, 18'8 and of the sovereignty and Independence of the United States of America the one hundred and Second

B F Kennedy PROTHONOTARY.

THE UNITED STATES OF AMERICA,

To all to whom these presents shall come, Greeting:

Homestead Certificate No. 3565

APPLICATION 5449 and 13930

Whereas There has been deposited in the General Land Office of the United States a Certificate of the Register of the Land Office at _Little Rock, Arkansas_, whereby it appears that, pursuant to the Act of Congress approved 20th May, 1862, "To secure Homesteads to actual Settlers on the Public Domain," and the acts supplemental thereto, the claim of _Ferdinand Kanis_ has been established and duly consummated, in conformity to law, for the _west half of the north east quarter of section eleven and the north east quarter of the south east quarter of the south west quarter and the south west quarter of the south east quarter of section two in township one north of range thirteen west of the Fifth Principal Meridian in Arkansas, containing one hundred and sixty_ Acres.

according to the Official Plat of the survey of the said Land, returned to the General Land Office by the Surveyor General:

Now know ye, That there is, therefore, granted by the United States unto the said _Ferdinand Kanis_ the tract of Land above described: TO HAVE AND TO HOLD the said tract of Land, with the appurtenances thereof, unto the said _Ferdinand Kanis_ and to _his_

In testimony whereof, I _____, President of the United States of America, have caused these letters to be made Office to be hereunto affixed.

Given under my hand, at the City of Washington, the _twentieth_ day of _June_ , in the year of our Lord one thousand eight hundred and _eighty five_ , and of the Independence of the United States the one hundred and _ninth_.

By the President: _M. M. Koran_

By _J. M. Heart_, Secretary.

Recorder of the General Land Office.

CERTIFICATE OF RECORD

STATE OF ARKANSAS, }
COUNTY OF PULASKI, } ss.

I, DAN. D. QUINN, Clerk of the Circuit Court and Ex-Officio Recorder, within and for said County, do hereby certify that the foregoing and annexed instrument of writing was filed in my office for record, on the _18_ day of _Nov._ A.D. 19_16_, at _11½_ o'clock _A._ M., and that the same is now duly recorded, with the acknowledgment and certificate thereon, in Record Book _123_ Page _253_.

IN TESTIMONY WHEREOF, I have hereunto set my hand and affixed my official seal, this the _18_ day of _Nov._ 19_16_.

Dan D. Quinn Clerk

By _T. E. Vaughter_ Deputy Clerk

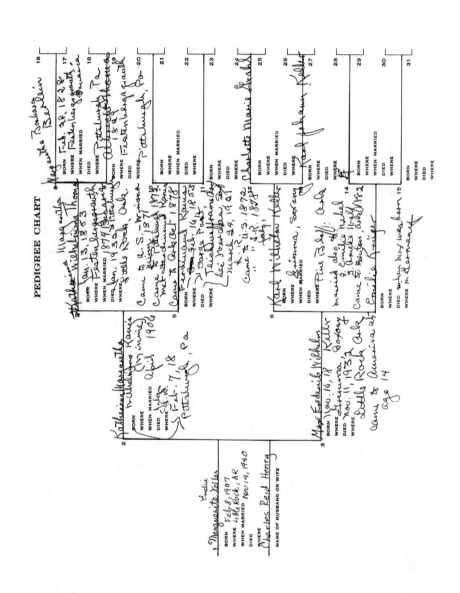

PEDIGREE CHART

1 Marguerite Keller
Emelia
BORN Feb. 8, 1907
WHERE Little Rock, AR
WHEN MARRIED Nov. 14, 1940
DIED
WHERE Charles Reid Henry

NAME OF HUSBAND OR WIFE

2 Katherine Margaretha
Wilhelmina Keues
BORN in mine
WHEN MARRIED April 1906
DIED Sept
WHERE Feb. 7, 18
Pittsburgh, Pa

3 Max Frederick Wilhelm
Keller
BORN Nov. 16, 18
WHERE Lüneberg, Germany
DIED Nov. 11, 1933
WHERE Little Rock, Ark
Came to America at
age 14

4 Katherine Margaretha Wilhelmina Thoma
BORN Jan. 13, 1853
WHERE Featonburgemauth
WHEN MARRIED 1874
DIED Jan. 19, 39 Little Rock, Ark.
WHERE
Came to U.S.—Winona
Came to Pittsburgh 1878
Met Ferdinand Keues
Came to Okt. Oct. 1878

5 Ferdinand Keues
BORN Jan. 14, 1853
WHERE Jorge Poole
DIED Tues One thousand
Joe Ferdinand Joy
March 24, 1941
Came to U.S. 1872
" " S.S. 1878.32

6 Karl Wilhelm Keller
BORN
WHERE Grimma, Saxony
WHEN MARRIED
DIED
WHERE Pine Bluff, Ark
married also, J. Emilie Nohel
3. Amelia Holl
Came to Bergen, 1882
Emilio Knight

7
BORN
WHERE
WHEN MARRIED
DIED
WHERE when they were born
WHERE in Germany

8 Margaretha Barbara Berlein
BORN Feb. 28, 1822
WHERE Featonburgemauth Germany
WHEN MARRIED
DIED Pittsburgh Pa
Oct 20 1903 Heepse
BORN 18 of Featonburgh, Pa
WHERE Featonburg Pa grand

	16
17	
18	
19	
20	
21	
22	
23	
24 Charlotte Marie Strahl	
25	
26 Karl Johann Keller	
27	
28	
29	
30	
31	

The Rocconi-Fratesi Family
Italianata In The Arkansas Delta

Amalite Fratesi, who has made and created things all her life — bread, wine, tortellini, children's stories, sketches, paintings, theatrical skits, arrangements of dried plants and flowers — has written what she terms a "true family history" of the Fratesi and Rocconi families. Intended for distribution only to family members, the account combines elements of historical fact, folk narrative, and morality tale. It describes emigrations and settlements, plantation tenancies, good and hard times, and infuses those descriptions with a sense of destiny and of what it has meant to be a Fratesi or a Rocconi in the south Arkansas delta. Separated by an ocean from ancestral villages and isolated as a minority in an alien and often hostile environment, the families persevered. Amalite writes: "My parents, the Rocconi's, and my husband's parents, the Fratesi's, were natives in near-by towns in Italy. They knew hardwork, hardships, disappointments in life. They were religious, they taught us to work and help carry family burdens from a very young age of 6 and 7...We were taught to take disappointments in life because they said that was to be expected ...

"I try to tell my children that life isn't always a 'bed of roses!' We do the best we can today, and ask God's help for the next: crop failures, low prices, sickness, droughts, wars; come and go by in through the years. We have survived! This has happened the past centuries. I'm sure it will happen in the future."

Those words not only express Amalite's belief in the continuity of her family but also reveal some of the values, attitudes, and outlooks upon which she feels that continuity must be based: tenacity, hard work, and faith, rooted in an Italian heritage. These are families whose *Italianata* has helped shape their ways of being American.

Family History. The Rocconi-Fratesi story begins in America with Ercola and Augusta Fratesi and Pietro and Julia Rocconi, who were among hundreds of Italians who emigrated early in this century to work Arkansas cotton plantations. The Fratesis arrived in 1906 from the Italian province of Pesaro. They worked as sharecroppers at New Gascony, near Pine Bluff, on a plantation owned by John Gracie. The Rocconis arrived in 1904 from the province of Ancona, and sharecropped on Redleaf plantation in Chicot County. The voyages from Italy, tangible manifestations of uprootings, are given shape as folk narrative by Amalite: "Ercola and his brother Joseppe came to America with their families in November in 1906. The voyage was taken in a very old ship by the name of *Queen Mary*. It took *Queen Mary* one month to cross the Atlantic Ocean to New York. It was known later that it was *Queen Mary's* last voyage. There were 3,500 passengers on board. Over 300 were Italian immigrants.

"My parents were Julia and Pietro. Julia was a Mazzanti who also lived in Ostra. They came to America in 1904. They borrowed 200 lires from Signor Cuicchi Achille. They married and came to America on their honeymoon; I presume my father came to America on the same ship. My Uncle Joe and Paul came to America two years later. The ship's name was Nord America. It took them 16 days to cross the ocean. The tickets to come to America was $54.00 — ½ price for children."

Details like the *Queen Mary* and the borrowing of "200 lires from Signor Cuicchi Achille" (whose name does not otherwise occur in the family stories) help give the history the air of an epic tale. In much the same vein, Amalite writes: "With the permission of Prince Ruspoli, Mayor of Italy; Mr. Gracie immigrated these Italian families to New Gascony" and "A millionaire, Austin Corbin; who lived in New York owned over 2,000 acres of this rich Delta land called Sunny Side. This land was worked and farmed with prisoners (Convicks). Austin Corbin while in Africa on a Jungle Hunt met a friend who told him about the Italians in Italy who were hard workers and good farmers."

Contrasts between Amalite's folk narrative and written historical data offer much about the function of family folklore. Written data indicates that Ruspoli was a mayor of Rome and that he served as Corbin's representative in Italy. There is no recorded connection in biographical accounts between him and Gracie. Nor is there any reference to a trip to Africa, where a scheme to employ Italian laborers on an Arkansas plantation was hatched by Corbin. Corbin, a millionaire and president of the Long Island Railroad in New York, did establish, before his death in 1897, a 26,000-acre game park in Newport, New Hamp-

The Rocconi children at Yellow Bayou. Amalite is on far left.

shire, that was 11 miles long and four miles wide. According to the *Dictionary of American Biography*, he "spent $1,000,000 stocking the preserve with animals and providing for their maintenance and increase."

Regarding Sunny Side, it covered about 11,000 acres in Chicot County and, under Corbin's ownership, constituted one of the most comprehensive attempts to establish a colony of immigrant Italian laborers in the rural South. The first Italians, about 100 families, arrived in 1895, and the plantation was farmed by Italians and Blacks for several years, although Corbin had used some convict labor before 1895. Sunny Side undoubtedly served as a model for the attempts by Gracie and the owners of Redleaf to attract Italian labor. For Italians who lived there, Sunny Side is remembered most for the large number, perhaps hundreds, of their people who died on the plantation as a result of malaria epidemics.

There were deaths from malaria at New Gascony and Redleaf also. Ercola and Augusta Fratesi lost a son and a daughter to the disease at New Gascony.

Economically, life was difficult for the immigrant families. After a few years at New Gascony that found them still in debt for their transatlantic boat fare, the Fratesis left for Sunny Side. A few years of financial failure there drove them to a section of Pine Bluff called "Dago Lane" (now Commerce Road), where several other Italian families had

In 1927 the teenage Amalite Rocconi turned an old gin receipt book into a scrapbook and diary. She drew pictures, pasted in snapshots and newspaper clippings, wrote observations and comments, and, in those ways, documented the lives of the Italian people around her in Chicot County.

Her drawings included one of a plantation manager telling why he couldn't eat food someone offered him (above) and several of flappers (facing page and chapter frontispiece). Amalite can be seen, third from left in the middle row, in the communion snapshot (facing page, top). The family snapshot (facing page, bottom) was taken, as Amalite's written comment explains, by Wine Fratesi, her future brother-in-law.

settled.

After a flood in 1912, the Rocconis left Redleaf for Memphis and Alabama, where Pietro found work in train-repair factories. He was laid off after some months and the family returned to Redleaf. In 1924, hoping for a better life, Pietro purchased 10 acres of land in Orlando, Florida. The family, including all eight children (each with a first name beginning with "A") packed their belongings and left Arkansas. Pietro could not find work in Orlando, however, and after only a few weeks the family moved to Sanford, Mississippi, where they were hired to work among a community of Sicilians on a strawberry farm. They remained there nine months before moving back to Arkansas and settling at Yellow Bayou in Chicot County. Those times made a strong impression on Amalite, who was 13 when her family left for Florida and Mississippi. She has written a brief story (published privately in Pine Bluff) about

That girl
has two fellers
no. you are
& mistaken
those are her
brothers. if

A Commun set
Can you find Rosalia Roccani &
I can.

THE FLOOD AT GREENEVILLE, MISS.

The flood in Greenville
lookes bad, but if you
was in yellow Bayou
when the flood was there
you would yell for help
thinking you were in a deluge.

I see nine persons but there is ten.
and I seen them. Can you? well I'll tell
you where the tenth is. You see the handle
well pete Roccani is holding. That's his
working Crew. Where is Vine. Hes snaping
the picture. I thought so. or else I knew he
would be close to his girl.

the trip entitled *My Mother's Rosary Beads*.

At Sanford, on the strawberry farm, Amalite's family stood out as quite different from the Sicilians around them. The Rocconis, very religious, wondered why the Sicilian people never attended Mass on Sundays. "My parents were very concerned about these people," Amalite writes. Her father arranged to drive a priest once a month to the strawberry farm from Hattiesburg, about 30 miles away, and her family cleaned a tenant house where the priest could celebrate Mass. From those acts Amalite has drawn a parallel: "Thirty years later, in Hattiesburg, my oldest daughter's husband was killed instantly in a three-car collision and my daughter was hospitalized there for three months. Life is a great puzzle. In that same town my father helped save souls.

"My daughter lives with me now and is known as a miracle girl. The doctors didn't expect her to live and if through a miracle she would survive she would be a vegetable. After a year or more with doctors and family love and care she made a wonderful recovery. When I think back God gave her back to us as a reward for my parents' accomplishments."

Perseverance. Although the Rocconis were "admired and loved" by the Sicilian families for a time, they later lost that admiration. Amalite and her brothers and sisters staged a small tent show: "Our neighbor had given us a baby billy goat. We taught him to sit at the table and drink milk out of a spoon and do other tricks. He was one of our main attractions. I had an old flowered kimono and also knew a little Japanese song, so my sisters and I made up a skit. I was the main character as a Japanese geisha girl. My father had in his possession a siren used in ambulances. We included some skits to use that. The show lasted one hour; admission was 25¢ ...

"We were astonished all the seats were taken. People were standing even on the outside of the tent. Our show was a success.

"From that moment we lost their admiration, gossip went around from house to house that we were gypsies and my mother a witch doctor because she healed one of the young girl's eyes. My mother only used some of our medicine that we took on the trip. Several doses cured this girl's eyes and other children's sores."

Despite those bad feelings, Amalite ends her account of her family's experience at Sanford with an emphasis on the amiability of their leave-taking: "We were amazed to see nearly all the families by the roadsides to bid us farewell. One of the women took mother's broom from among the furniture in the trailer. 'Taking a broom with you when you move brings bad luck,' she yelled as we moved on.

"Mother had tears in her eyes. 'Piee (Pietro), they didn't dislike us. Down deep in their hearts they hate to see us leave.'

"It's a wonderful feeling to know we won their love."

The sense of separation and isolation and the lessons of perseverance, faith and hard work associated with these and other family ex-

(Above) The Fratesi living room during a recent Christmas. (Left) Amalite holding a photograph of herself and Dan.

periences pervade not only Amalite's family narrative and her account of the 1924 trip, but also two children's stories she has written. "Frizzle's Adventure" concerns a funny-looking, industrious chick who is taken from her Mother Hen, brother and sister chicks, and barnyard companions to a new farm. There none of the animals like her and she is attacked by bugs and mites. She escapes as thieves rob the chicken house, but, attempting to find her way home, she becomes lost in a forest. In a hollow tree, quite afraid and running out of courage, she encounters a wounded goose who sings:

> "Let's all be happy,
> Let's all be true.
> Let's pack all our troubles away
> All the day through.
> And let's always hope for the best
> While our short lives last!"

It's Frizzle's song, and only someone who had been to her home could have heard it. She nurses the goose to health, and he flies her home where she is reunited with her family and friends.

The second story, "The Adventures of Jolly Jim, the Grasshopper," concerns a fiddle-playing grasshopper who leaves his home in search of perennially warm and verdant paradise. He undertakes the journey alone, but with the hope and purpose of improving and extending life for all his tribe of grasshoppers. After much persistence and many trials, including a ship-wreck, he arrives in South America, fulfilling his dream. (There is a parallel in this story: Amalite's aunt — her mother's sister Theraza — left Italy for South America years ago and the family

91

lost contact with her.)

Traditions. The traditions binding both the Fratesi and Rocconi families have been integral to farm life and working on the land. In Italy, Ercola Fratesi farmed and tended oxen, and Pietro Rocconi, although not a farmer, thrashed wheat and repaired farm machinery.

In America, Ercola, tending mules at first, settled into farming, as did his three sons, Nick, Dan, who married Amalite, and Geurrino, called Wine, who married Amalite's older sister Angelina. Pietro farmed only briefly at Redleaf; for the most part, he made a living as a blacksmith, mechanic, and carpenter. His five sons did farm, however. And Dan and Amalite's two sons, Harry and Benny, both farm. Benny, who has a degree in agriculture from the University of Arkansas, has become a leading spokesman for the American Agriculture Movement, and in testimony before a congressional committee in Washington, D.C. about the plight of family farmers, he communicated an appreciation of his own family tradition when he told of his grandfather's experience as a sharecropper at New Gascony.

The Fratesi and Rocconi families became connected in the late 1920s when Angelina and Wine and then Dan and Amalite were married. The two young brides moved in with their husbands' parents on the Fratesis' 120-acre farm in Pine Bluff. Amalite describes that situation in an interview: " ... now my parents didn't believe in that. They were from Italy and everything but they still didn't believe in that. They said that, 'Once you kids get married I want you to make your own homes.' Because it's just problems and it's too hard to live, you know, too many families in one place. But my husband's parents, oh wee!, they really believed in not letting the children leave home. They just actually believed you're supposed to live there all together no matter how many brothers — well now the daughters would leave but the sons all had to remain there — no matter how many brothers there were, you were supposed to live there with them until they passed away. And if you owned anything, nothing was anybody's but theirs until they passed away ... At one time we were, let's see, my sister and I, and they even took in the daughter and her husband ... which we were four families living in the same house ... It was a six-room house. There was four bedrooms and the dining room and the kitchen and that was it. And then we had long halls in between and the porches on the side. And the children slept in one room." (Note: Amalite says that Nick, older brother to Dan and Wine, "couldn't get along or agree with his parents' ideas" (presumably about living under one roof), and left home to farm on his own in the area. After an initial period of strained relations, Nick and his parents were on good terms.)

Amalite was married in Lake Village (the town nearest Yellow Bayou, Redleaf, and Sunny Side) when she was 17 by Father J. F. Galloni, a parish priest who was a close friend of the Rocconis and of

A painting by Amalite depicts a time when a dove fry was an annual autumn event for the Fratesi family and their friends. Doves were hunted in the morning and early afternoon, and the fry took place in late afternoon — all at the Fratesi land in Lincoln County. Although Benny and his friends still have a dove hunt and fry, the event is no longer a family affair for the Fratesis.

most Italian families in the area. (According to Amalite, it was Fr. Galloni who suggested that Pietro and Julia give all of their children names beginning with "A".)

"Our honeymoon was just worrying," Amalite recalls, "driving in the car up here...that was our trip. And they still have that custom...It was so ridiculous — that's worse than some fables that you read somewhere — but did you know that the mother-in-law was the last to leave our bedroom. She would come in — you know we didn't have electric lights then; we had a lamp — she would come in, when we'd give her permission to come in, and blow out the light and give our blessing. But she would come *in* that room, put the light out ... "

Augusta, Dan's mother, was renowned for her abilities as a midwife. According to Amalite, Augusta never lost a baby or a mother in the years she practiced among the Italian people in New Gascony, Sunny Side, and Pine Bluff: "In Italian they called her mamana...I remember any time during the night or in the day, anywhere, they (the Italians) would come get her with wagons or, later on, with the car. And she would be gone all night and come back, and she said, 'Everything's fine.' And they wouldn't give her, they wouldn't pay her. She wouldn't ask for anything, so they would give her material to make a dress, or maybe a pair of chickens. Sometime, nothing. You know, they couldn't afford it. And she would deliver these children, and then go back once or twice to see how the mother was getting along. But she is the mother of all these Italians. All these ... that are still here now."

Amalite never saw her mother-in-law deliver a baby, but she recalls that Augusta used no medicines and would sometimes say prayers and light a candle to the Virgin Mary before leaving for a delivery. Curiously, Julia Rocconi, Amalite's mother, did not allow Augusta to deliver Amalite's children. Amalite remembers her mother saying to Augusta: "That's one thing we're gonna make agreement on — you're not gonna deliver any of my daughter's children." However, while she was still living, Augusta was present in the room when the doctor delivered Amalite's children.

During the 1930s and early 1940s, when Amalite was having her four children, childbirth was a significant event for Italian families in the Pine Bluff area. After giving birth, mothers were given a 40-day rest, during which time they remained inside the home, were not expected to do housework, and ate only chicken broth and soup. "I didn't mind when the children came 'cause I got a rest," Amalite says. "For 40 days they didn't let us do anything. We were queens. Really." Italian neighbors would bring a hen or two, or fruit if they had no hens, to the new parents. Baptisms, which were generally celebrated a week after births, were occasions for feasting — although mothers remained at home and did not attend the church service; babies were taken to church by fathers and godparents.

Weddings were perhaps the most celebrated and memorable special occasions. Amalite recalls Fratesi family weddings: "When the oldest son married — Nick — they actually fixed — they had an old, I guess it was a two-room house on the place — well, just in the yard, not far from the house. They fixed that and broke down the walls and made it one big room where they actually feasted and ate for one week ... It lasted one week and I just can't imagine how they fed hundreds of ... All the Italians that they knew went. And they had just — they made their own wine, they made their own beer. They raised their own chickens for the feast. And all of them would pitch in and clean these, dress these chickens, you know, for the wedding...Now when the next brother married — Wine — it lasted about three or four days. And when Dan and I married it didn't last but a couple of days."

Augusta died in 1937. After Ercola died in 1940, Dan and Amalite and Wine and Angelina divided the family land in half, built twin houses, and shared a single barn. In 1943, however, a flood along the Arkansas River destroyed Dan and Amalite's home, wrecked Wine and Angelina's home, and ruined the land for farming. For Amalite, the disaster marked the loss of a financial and emotional independence she had gained after having lived with her husband's parents for so long: "And we just stuck it out and stuck it out and stuck it out until they passed away. And then we divided up after they passed away. We tore the old house up and got some of the lumber from that. And Wine — we divided the land in half — and Wine built a home in a half of it and Dan built a home on the other half...So we just divided. But then when this flood came there was nothing to divide. The land was just ruined and washed and gullies. Our home was washed away. But Wine's home was not. His was left on a little hill and his part of the land wasn't ruined as bad as ours. There was no chance of...oh, we just couldn't think of going back. There was nothing to go back to."

Following the flood Dan and Amalite moved to another part of Pine Bluff and sharecropped for nine months. Their crop failed because of drought. But with the aid of the Red Cross they were able to make a down payment on 40 acres of land in Pine Bluff and to add one room to a house that stood on that land.

Prosperity gradually came. Dan farmed rented acreage in addition to his own land each year and did well. In 1945 the Fratesis opened a general store that filled the needs of their Italian and Black neighbors. In 1953 they had a new home built on their 40 acres. In 1960 they bought over 600 acres in Lincoln County, and later they operated a 60-unit trailer park near their home.

Dan and Amalite retired in 1971, although Dan still does some farm work with Benny, who has bought his parents' Lincoln County land. Since their retirement they have made three trips to Italy.

Through the years many changes in Fratesi family traditions and practices have taken place. Celebrations — baptisms, for instance, and weddings — aren't the enormous, lengthy communal occasions they once were. Women no longer take 40 days rest after giving birth. Bocce, the Italian lawn bowling game, is played only infrequently. Italian is no longer spoken by the younger generation, and intermarriage with non-Italians is common.

Holidays. Holidays are still times for three generations of the family to gather at Dan and Amalite's house, however. Easter, Thanksgiving, and Christmas, especially, are highlighted by the serving of a meal featuring traditional Italian cooking. (One change in the family's holiday eating pattern has been the elimination of *lupini* beans, black olives and anchovies that were traditionally eaten in the days before Christmas — they have now become too difficult to obtain.) At Easter Amalite makes a special bread with raisins and orange and lemon peels, and family members each eat a boiled, blessed egg before attending Mass. Amalite then holds an egg hunt for the family and neighbor children, and members of the family participate in folk drama — wearing bunny suits, they act out skits invented by Amalite.

Food remains an important part of life for the Fratesis. Amalite

Hard-Crusted Bread

The isolation of being Italian in a strange country was experienced firsthand by Dan Fratesi. He tells a story, remembered from his childhood, about how he was treated as an Italian boy going to school in Pine Bluff: "Well, when we first came to this country, they weren't friendly at all. We'd go to school, and they'd call you Dago and they'd try to fight you and try to chunk a rock, try to throw a brick at you, and other things...And even when we'd get out from school, and we'd have to fight every day just about. And so, one — it was a cripple man too, a Catholic — and he was, he would load up a book sack full of brick and then he'd chase us with the horse. He'd chase us. He'd throw rocks and bricks at us. So, one of the boys one day they had a fight, you know, and they had the bread they cooked in the oven, used to cook — not in the pan but right on top of the brick in these ovens — and they'd keep them about, oh, they'd cook every week, you know, and the bread'd get hard. And, you know the end of the bread, you know, it'd get just like a brick. So when he got angry, you know, with some boys and so he got that piece of bread and it just knocked the fool out of him just like a rock. And so he went in the schoolhouse and crying and hollering and says, 'They chucked me a brick. He knocked me down with a brick, he hit me.' He said, 'No, it wasn't no brick. It was a piece of bread.' (Laughs) They got that piece of bread and they went to gnawing, gnawing on it just like it was, just like a bone, you know, hard...gnaw on it, instead of biting it — you couldn't bite it, it was too hard. He said, 'How can you eat this bread?' He said he showed him how to eat it, you know."

(Far left) Amalite opening an old brick oven formerly used for making bread and for roasting meats. The oven, owned by the Aureli family of Pine Bluff, is quite similar to those used by the Fratesis and other Italian families in the area.
(Left) Pasta drying in the Fratesi kitchen.

regularly makes her own bread and *sfoglia*, flour and egg pasta. She cuts the pasta into spaghetti and also uses it as the dough for her tortellini and ravioli. She fills the tortellini with Parmesan cheese, celery, onion, lemon juice, lemon rind, nutmeg, and finely chopped pork, beef, and chicken. The ravioli filling is similar, although the meats are boiled and neither nutmeg nor lemon is added. Amalite makes wines from Concord grapes and other fruits. She cooks squab that Dan raises and dove, rabbit, and other game caught by Benny and other family members. Each winter the family makes *lonza*, cured pork loin, which they eat throughout the year. Dan braids and dries garlic he grows, and tends a garden, where vegetables are grown for home use and, when overabundant, for roadside sale. In season, vegetables from that home garden form the basis for the salads that the family eats regularly at dinners with an oil and vinegar dressing.

Dan and Amalite are also active in their local Catholic church, and Amalite often prepares Italian dishes for church affairs.

But perhaps more than any other single thing, their extended-family life occupies Dan and Amalite and continues to provide purpose for their achievements and difficulties and a context for their traditions. Three of their children live close to them, including Mary Louise, who lives at home. In Pine Bluff they frequently visit Wine and Angelina as well as another of Amalite's sisters, Amalia, and her husband, Robert Ruggeri. They also stay in regular contact with Amalite's brothers in Lake Village. On their most recent trip to Italy, accompanied by their grandniece Deborah, they revisited Amalite's relatives.

It is family life approached with the spirit of generations in Italian villages, tempered by the experience of more than 75 years on Arkansas farms. And it has been concern for the continuity of that spirit — as well as personal resourcefulness and creativity — that has led Amalite to write her family history. She ends that account: "A request: Please don't

Making Lonza

Louis: How (do you) make your lonza?

Amalite: Now that's ... that lonza, really, I think, you know, the Italians brought that recipe from Europe, from Italy. Because, you know, the Italians made it from when they first came over to America. They all raised their own hogs, and that's the way we did it then. We raised, you know, back there, you raised your own hogs and then got the pork loin out of them, when you cut the hog up. But now we don't raise them. I just go to...a meat place, a meat-packing place, and just buy the leanest pork loins that I can find. You know, they're cut into whole loins. And then I cut, we cut it, cut the bone out, and just leave this loin in one long piece. And we salt it down for, oh...well, you salt it down — we have a table that you put salt underneath and then you put salt all around — you completely cover your loin with salt. For three days...I use that Morton salt. It is a table salt but it's a...canning salt, pickling salt, you know, that doesn't have anything in it but that salt, coarse-looking salt. It's a little coarser. And after it's been under salt for the three days, you take it and wash it in warm water and vinegar. You wash all that salt off real good. Then you beat it up. You have to have — we use a large rolling pin — you beat it in order to break the muscles and where it will be tender when you eat it, you know. It tenderizes — I guess that's what it's for. And you use a cheesecloth like that, and you season it with — I wet my cloth with pure vinegar — I use that apple cider vinegar, the strong vinegar — and that — you notice that pepper's a little coarse — you use that coarse pepper — and garlic — you chop garlic up — you can't tell it, but it's garlic in there, and pepper. And you wrap it up and tie it like that. After you beat it, beat it up, beat your loins up real tender — and then you roll it up in this cloth and put the seasoning around it... You put the seasoning inside, and then roll it. And then you let it — you do that, we usually do it in January when it's cool, you know, and let it hang, you know, airy place, inside of a building. We have this building back here that we — a kitchen we call — used to be my canning kitchen, when all the children were home. But, anyway, it will take about two months to cure like that.

Louis: That's the whole tenderloin?

Amalite: Yes. The whole tenderloin.

Louis: Do you process it all in one piece?

Amalite: All in one piece... And then when it's, when you know it's cured, you don't leave it hanging there. Because if you do, it'll get so ranky and dry, you can't eat it. So then I just cut it in parts and put it in a plastic bag and freeze it. Put it in my deep freeze. So that way it'll stay fresh, you know, long as you have it, all the time.

Dan and Amalite's grandchildren, Dusty Fratesi, Dean Allen McGhee and Dusty Shannon McGhee, performing one of Amalite's Easter skits without bunny suits.

let this family history die. Before each one of you get too old continue what we have started. God bless all of you and keep you, your mother, Amalite Fratesi."   —Louis Guida

PEDIGREE CHART

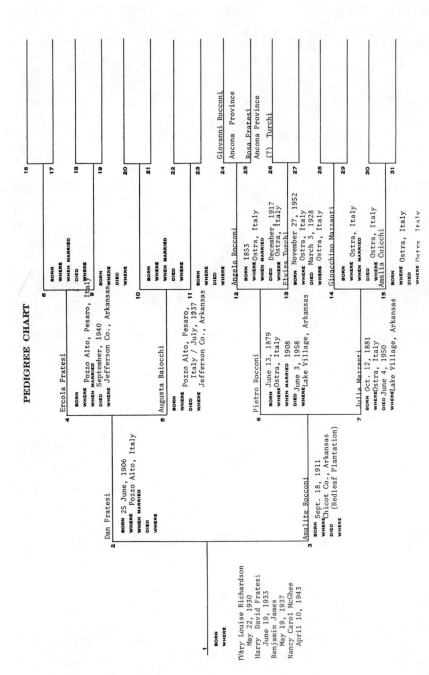

8

16

17

4 Ercola Fratesi

18

BORN
WHERE Pozzo Alto, Pesaro, Italy
WHEN MARRIED
DIED September, 1940
WHERE Jefferson Co., Arkansas

19

9

2 Dan Fratesi

20

BORN 25 June, 1906
WHERE Pozzo Alto, Italy
WHEN MARRIED
DIED
WHERE

10

21

5 Augusta Baiocchi

22

BORN
WHERE Pozzo Alto, Pesaro,
DIED Italy / July, 1937
WHERE Jefferson Co., Arkansas

11

23

24 Giovanni Rocconi
Ancona Province

12 Angelo Rocconi

25 Rosa Fratesi
Ancona Province

BORN 1853
WHERE Ostra, Italy
WHEN MARRIED
DIED December, 1917
WHERE Ostra, Italy

26 (?) Turchi

6 Pietro Rocconi

13 Elvira Turchi

27

BORN June 13, 1879
WHERE Ostra, Italy
WHEN MARRIED 1908
DIED June 3, 1958
WHERE Lake Village, Arkansas

BORN November 27, 1952
WHERE Ostra, Italy
DIED March 3, 1928
WHERE Ostra, Italy

28

3 Amalite Rocconi

14 Gioacchino Mazzanti

29

BORN Sept. 18, 1911
WHERE Chicot Co., Arkansas
DIED (Redleaf Plantation)
WHERE

BORN
WHERE Ostra, Italy
WHEN MARRIED
DIED Ostra, Italy
WHERE Ostra, Italy

30

7 Julia Mazzanti

15 Amalia Cuicchi

31

BORN Oct. 12, 1881
WHERE Ostra, Italy
DIED June 4, 1950
WHERE Lake Village, Arkansas

BORN
WHERE Ostra, Italy
DIED
WHERE Ostra, Italy

1

BORN
WHERE

Mary Louise Richardson
May 22, 1930
Harry David Fratesi
June 19, 1933
Benjamin James
May 19, 1937
Nancy Carol McGhee
April 10, 1943

The Johnson-Tolefree Family
"We've Got Hogs in the Bottom"

Every year the children pursued a private, annual ritual. It took place on Christmas Day at sundown, as the Johnson women were carrying leftovers to the kitchen and the men were stuffing paper and string into the sitting-room stove. The youngsters would save a paper bag from the stove's flames, and with serious expression drop their candy inside. A twist at the top transformed the bag into a candy man who would for days to come prolong the sweetness of Christmas.

A few hours earlier the room had resounded with the confident, measured steps of their mother Lemma, who filled the table with boiled hen, ham, dressing, potato salad, collard greens, and jam cake with caramel icing: all standard Christmas fare. Santa Claus had come. His work, the six Johnson children knew, was done in a prescribed order. Noiselessly, he cut all the pies and cakes; then he parcelled out the candy, nuts, and fruit; finally, he placed a few gifts on the tree and on the floor around it. "If you were bad," recalls the youngest daughter Linda Tolefree, "Santy Claus wouldn't come to see you, and if you were awake, he'd throw ashes in your eyes." Most years, Lemma's people came to eat and watch the children open gifts. All day long, friends entered, intoned greetings, had a snack, joked and talked, then went away.

For days thereafter the candy man would occupy a corner in the Johnson sitting room. From there he had full view of the polished, jagged foliage of the holly Christmas tree. The children were not concerned by his contrasting shabbiness; for every withdrawal from the

(Left) Lemma Johnson, shown by her daughter Linda Tolefree, worked as a domestic for most of her life. (Above) Santa Claus entertains the Tolefree twins Kelly (l.) and Jeanelle (r.).

collected hoard would echo Santa's blessings from an all-providing source. There was a game implicit in this ritual. Once a child put in his share, he earned a license to challenge the others that *HE could HAVE howEVa MUCH he WONT*. A verbal duel ensued. Then an outright charge of excess greed. Last, a swift retort which, according to custom, never failed to silence the accusers. "I've got HOGS in the BOTtom," the triumphant plunderer would cry. "It meant," Linda said, "that whenever you started out with somethin', you could eat until it was all gone, even if you didn't have but one piece!"

Hogs and Men. As a folk expression, "hogs in the bottom" refers to the infinite resources of nature. "Yes," her father Ivan Johnson concurred with a chuckle. "If [anybody] had a hog in the bottom, he always DID have a hog in there. This year he kill ever' one he had; next year he have a claim in the bottom, he go back there and kill him some MORE hogs." As a welcome addition to the diet, candy and hogs have much in common; but in about every other way, they are plainly different. The joke in the children's game turns on a false analogy that credits candy with the mysterious power of increase found in hogs.

The saying "hogs in the bottom" was passed down because hogs were important to sawmill men like Ivan Johnson. They drew not only their livelihood but also their meat from the woodlands around Banks and Warren. Ivan Johnson likes to talk about hogs. "In those times," he explains, "they had them hogs runnin' loose in the woods, jus' anybody's hogs, jus' goin' down killin' some hogs jus' like we killin' rabbits and squirrels now." Acorns and hickory nuts supplied the animals with plenty of mash. Since each family's hogs chose a regular feeding place, it was easy to send out the dogs to "scent them up." As soon as a dog got a good grip on a pig, the victim's squeals called others in his direction. The dogs would "bay 'em" and then chase them "on home." Contrary to the fiction that hogs were public property, a farmer generally tried to mark his young ones once a year. Ivan's mark was "smooth off to the left, over half to the right." This meant that any hog having only a bottom right ear remaining belonged to him. Once the hogs were caught, Ivan might pen them for weeks or even months depending on how fat he wanted them to be. But he never butchered them except on the waning of the moon. That way, he believed, the fat would cook out better.

Hogs, so important to the family in practical life, also had a place in the family philosophy. Metaphorically, the expression "hogs in the bottom" describes the inexhaustible resilience of man. To say "I've got hogs in the bottom" means in this sense "I can do whatever I wish with the talents I was born with." At the age of 80, Ivan Johnson still teaches his children and grandchildren that whatever abilities they started with will stay with them throughout their lives. External limits, he believes, will never curb the power of a self-replenishing human will.

Traditional family lore reinforces this lesson in stories that follow a single, repeated pattern. They begin with an ancestor or relative who appears as a lonely figure set against a hard, irrational world. This protagonist might be Aunt Alice, who spent her days in slavery fruitlessly jumping up and down to entertain a white child (see "Jump Up Alice," pg. 106); Uncle Orange, who posed as a "nigger-killer" to gain his co-workers' respect (see "Uncle Orange, the 'Nigger Killer,'" below); Ivan himself, who was called into forced labor on Bradley County roads in the Depression years. As the story develops, the person may "put

Uncle Orange, The "Nigger-Killer"_____

This is a Johnson family tale about Ivan's Uncle Orange who left home to work in another town. His co-workers greeted him, a stranger, with such hostility that he was driven to pose as an escaped criminal from the state of Louisiana. "Markin' no time," a phrase that appears in the story, refers to the straw-boss who marks in a notebook the hours each man works.

Ivan: I had 'n uncle aroun' Fordyce. Said time got so TOUGH aroun' Fordyce couldn't hardly make a livin'. So he lef' Fordyce then and went up on the Cotton Belt, went to workin' for the Cotton Belt Lumber Company. Said he didn't know much to do. Said the guy was sort of a half straw-boss. [The uncle] said, "Mister, can you please tell me what the Capt'n said to do?" The ol' guy raise up an' laugh, "O ho ho ho! I ain't markin' no time. Take your trouble to the Captain." He went all over 'em [asking the same question and getting the same reply.] Finally, he said, "Look here ol' nigger. You don't know me how come me here." Said the man looked up. "How come I'm here? For KILLIN' So-and-so's. This is not my home, LOUISIANA'S my home!"

Aw, from then on had a mighty good time on the Cotton Belt. Nigger'd be raisin' rough house 'n see me comin'. [In a whispering, excited voice] "Yall! Ol' Louisiana! Y'all! Ol' Louisiana!" [It was so quiet] You could hear chance crawlin' on the cotton!

down" his oppressors through a verbal or gestural trick, or he may choose willingly to comply and endure. But in either instance he never sheds his cool, detached perspective. Rather, he recognizes the irony of his situation and responds in a manner that safeguards his personal integrity. Here is a vision of man as a thinking being capable of transcending his oppression. By granting man intellectual control over external events, it has greater psychological force than a vision borne of anger and blame.

For the Johnsons these stories are the touchstones that define their inner worth. Experience has taught them that human acts are frequently unpredictable and wrong-headed. In a world often turned askew by selfishness, arrogance, and hate, it would be an error to measure oneself against the opinions of others. Ivan's word for this darker side of human nature is "yippie." It means "irrational" or "unthinking." "Yippie-ness" in his philosophy is a given, unpredictable force in human

"Jump Up Alice"_____

Among the stories black mothers pass down to their daughters are tales about slavery. This one entered the Johnson family through Linda's maternal grandmother, Texas Florence Hines. Here it is transcribed in two versions, the first told by Linda Tolefree and the second by her father, Ivan Johnson.

Linda: Aunt Alice lived during slavery time. And the people who owned her had a little girl. And that little girl was crying and carrying on. And so in order to pacify the little girl, Alice jumped up a couple of times. And the little girl thought that was the most wonderful thing. So, every time Aunt Alice would stop, she'd say, "Jump up, Alice." And Alice would jump up some more. This went on for hours and hours. So finally, Aunt Alice tried to pretend and ignore the little girl. She said [in a very high voice,] "Jump Alice." Aunt Alice couldn't jump. And the owner said [in a hard, rapid voice], "Jump up, Alice. You hear Mistress talking to you." So, poor Aunt Alice spent the day jumping up and down to please that little girl.

Ivan: My wife's grandmother said in slave times she was a house girl. She tended the baby. Says she was so worried when the Ole Missus come in. Missus took the baby, and she says she was so worried and tired she just jumped up. Said that little baby "jumped" her and broke her down. Said every time she'd quit, "Jump up Alice, jump up. Jump up, Alice, jump up." Said she'd jump, jump. She'd quit. The Mama said, "You hear her talking to you. Jump up, jump up there Alice." Said when she quit jumping she was washed down in sweat, jumping up for that little baby.

Deirdre: What do you make of that story?

Linda: Well, I think I'd have rather jumped up than do a lot of other things she'd probably would have had to have done if she hadn't been jumpin'!

Deirdre: Why do you think that story was handed down?

Linda: It was the idea of taking orders from a baby...and such a RIDICULOUS order!

Deirdre: Where did this take place?

Linda: Well, as far as I can understand it, it happened in Bradley County, down around Hermitage someplace.

psychology and in the society humans make for themselves. The stories show that where yippie-ness reigns, cool intelligence is the only adequate counterforce; for, intelligence keeps one's "hogs in the bottom" by preserving one's inner resources. An ideal balance between yippie and cool is the cornerstone of the Johnsons' world view. It underpins their stories, guides their lives, and shapes their attitudes toward the family past.

Up From Slavery. The most yippie American institution of all was slavery, and the oldest ancestor the Johnson family can remember is

---

Johnson Family Words And Expressions

Every family has a glossary of words and expressions that raise a chuckle or put forward a privately-held idea. In the case of the Johnsons, sisters, cousins, uncles, or parents recognize this special vocabulary as a token of their relationship as kin. A few terms ("J.W.E.'s" and "Jippies," for example) have found their way into the group through the creative imaginations of individual members. Readers from the Delta will understand others as expressions that circulate region-wide. Whatever its origin, family speech evolves through a constant process of selection that makes habits out of certain terms. Like a familiar melody, they enter the conversation laden with the remembered utterance of many speakers, and for those who know them well, they bind family members in the present with members from the past.

J.W.E.'s	girl's panties
JIPPIES	Long John's (long underwear)
YIPPIE	irrational, unreasonable (usually referring to one person's behavior toward another)
For her he CARRIED HIS STOOL AND SAT ON IT.	He went out of his way to do something for her; he gave her problem long and close attention.
I'm FRIENDLY today.	Today I have money to spend.
a BIG NICKLE	an ample backside
He's JULIUS.	He's wary.
He LICKED HER IN.	He finally got her to marry him.
"LET'S CALL IN THE DOGS."	We may as well give up hope of going anywhere tonight.
She's GONE TO THE PEN.	She's delivering a child.
I'm FOXY!	extremely hungry
She ATE IT ON LONG TEETH.	She ate it gingerly (because she thought it was unclean, foul-tasting, unusual, or spoiled).
He really PUT THE BIG POT INSIDE THE LITTLE ONE.	He pulled off a coup, achieved a achieved a great success.

107

Henry Johnson, a slave. He experienced bondage and the more difficult years following Emancipation. Ivan tells that his grandfather Henry "walked" from West Virginia to Arkansas — or at least to the market where he was sold. He married his wife Julie when he reached his new home.

Ivan's paternal grandmother was from Alabama, and she met her husband from West Virginia in Union County, Arkansas. Ivan explained: "Well, you know, [in a matter-of-fact tone] at that time we were sold. That's how it come up. They met in Union County. The Old Boss Man bought both of them ... Billy Boswell. He was the highest bidder. She sold for $1400 and he sold for $1200. Girls always brought more than boys. [He paused to visualize the scene.] Short dresses...short sleeves ... standin' on the sell block."

Though his grandparents "done passed long, LONG time," Ivan can still evoke their presence through bits of legend that cling loosely to the all-but-faded image of them he holds in his mind's eye. Men and women around Lanark, the Johnson homeplace, claimed that Henry was a remarkable reaper of rye, wheat, and oats: "Back then they had this ol' hand thing. They called it a 'cradle.' And all of them say, 'Henry Johnson was a CRADLER.' He could get a job anywhere, stay with anybody 'cause he could cradle. They say he could really use that cradle. He cradled his own farm and he cradled the white folks' farm."

However skilled Henry might have been, he couldn't make a living after Emancipation hiring out as a cradler. Unless he had a bit of cash saved up, sharecropping was a man's only option in the rural districts. Ivan describes Henry's transition from slavery to sharecropping in classic terms: "The ol' Boss Man, he took 'em in. He give 'em the tools 'n the stock 'n all, an' he give 'em half of what they can make. That was pretty good. You see, they didn't have NUTHIN'. My folks didn't have NUTHIN'."

No one knows exactly how old Henry was then, but it is plain that he was married and had children. Ivan surmises that his family continued some form of sharecropping on the Boswell farm for ten or more years until his grandfather was able to save enough to set up a forty-acre homestead in Bradley County, at Lanark: "He proved it up down at Camden. They call it 'provin' it up.' Built a house, cleared some ground. They built some little log huts. They dig a well. They have a house raisin'. And they'd have a breakdown that night. Say [he laughs] that would settle the house. Music? Aw, they'd fiddle. Them ol' men could

Ghost Stories _____

A favorite Johnson family pastime is swapping tales about the mischievous "hants" who provoke harmless accidents around the household. Their devilment is a source of nervous amusement for family members who half believe these ghostly capers. Each fresh report of strange goings-on offers mounting evidence that these spirits might, after all, genuinely exist.

The author of these stories is Ivan Johnson. His "Money Hunting" tale describes a "true" event that took place about forty years ago. By now, it has passed into the family repertoire, and the version recorded here is told by his daughter Linda.

The Money Hunters and the Hant

Deirdre: What did you grow back then?

Ivan: Well ... cotton, corn, peanuts ... that way back stuff ... cotton, corn, peanuts ... sorghum. You want somethin' good, you get some of that homemade sorghum syrup. [Introducing story] The old men had another pretty good harvest: huntin' money. They thought there was lots of money here, you know, when the Civil War came, lots of the men went off to fight and buried the money and never did get back. Probably got killed or something. And some of them found money, too. It all be gold.

Linda: [Tells Ivan's story] One man named Lee McHenry and ... I don't remember what the other man's name was ... anyway, it was rumored that there was money buried over there where Daddy had a field once. So people used to go around asking people to dig money on their land, and if they found money they were, of course, supposed to give the landowner however much they were going to give him.

So, Lee and his brother went over there that night to get the money. And they dug into a pit. I don't remember what the dimensions were, but anyway it was lined with brick from one end to the other and had a brick floor. And they were diggin' and diggin' and just about to get the money. And they say that when you find buried treasure, if you talk, then the money will go away.

One of the two of them said something. Something came out of the woods and jumped on the two men and beat them half to death. [Much laughter.] [And when the men told Daddy he said] "Did it HURT him? Did it HURT him? Did it HURT him?" "Did it HURT HIM??? [They responded.] It like to BREAK HIS NECK." And then he went across the field saying, "Goody, goody, goody, goody." This was the hant that went across the field saying, "Goody, goody, goody, goody. Goody, goody, goody, goody." [laughs.]

(Other stories are of recent origin and feature a "hant" who makes periodic rounds of the house; signs of his presence are a banging front door, a faint breeze circulating through the living room and kitchen, and a creaking rocking chair on the front porch. He is easily embarrassed if caught in the act of making trouble. The only person who has seen him clearly is daughter Ola Mae.)

The New Hant

Ivan: I was up there on the back porch one day shelling peas, and I heard him when he throwed the pan down. And I got up and come and I looked and I looked.

Well, a few more days I was back there shelling peas. And he throwed the pan down, and I ran there real quick. He didn't have time to get that up ... that big ol' white dish pan. So, he didn't have time to get that up, and he hasn't been back since. I LIKE to CAUGHT him! That's a real ol'-timey hant!

Ivan: I never did see him. I was sittin' out there on the porch one night by myself, and a car came back from up that way, and it had two lights. When I tried to hit on him [his form could be seen in the light], the lights was gone. I never did see him no more.

FIDDLE, too!

Sharecroppers "on the fourth" waited a long time before establishing their own farms. What was the system like? In Ivan's historical vision, past and present share common features: "Jus' like, let's say y'all had me and my family, and we'd all work two and two and y'all'd give me a fourth of what I made. See, y'all done the work, we done the work. You'd give us a fourth of what we made."

Julie Johnson outlived her husband by many years, and as a child Ivan saw her split rails, plough, and tend the farm. "She was pretty tight on little children," he recalls with a chuckle, but he remembers her best for the name she gave his father. He tells a story about it: "My daddy was born in the days of freedom. Long about that time ... freedom. She wanted to name him Abraham Lincoln, but the Ku Klux found out about it. Puttin' that strop on 'em. So she never did name him Abraham Lincoln. They called him 'Billy' until he was grown. Then she named him Elijah, 'Lidge' Lincoln. They had to have some of it. Elijah Lincoln, that was my dad's name."

A One-Mule Farm. After Henry's death Elijah stayed in the little Lanark Community to farm his father's land. His wife was Eliza Chives, a neighbor girl who gave birth to their eleven children. It was an unwritten rule that each child have a special family nickname. Ella was called "Monk," Widdie Troy was "Wid," Cornelius "Hock," Lettie "Let," Pink Marshall "Boot," and Ivan "Bud." The only exceptions were Lee Roy, Ivan's next youngest brother, the twins Ever and Everlina, who died in infancy, and sister Hattie Mae. Later, Ivan's wife Lemma would dub him "Ivory," her own embroidered corruption of his given name. Pink is the topic of a family story in which a white woman remarked on hearing the name "Pink Marshall:" "Well, you're the ugliest, blackest Pink I ever seen in my life!"

Elijah's farm, like Ivan's in later years, was self-sustaining. Handles for tools were hewn at home; mule muzzles were made of heavy steel wire; dresses and quilts were sewn from cloth that underwent myriad transformations before finishing their lives as rags. Occasionally the brothers and sisters rescued a remnant to make clothing for the dolls they fashioned from sticks and string ("Children's Games, at right). Family water dippers, in Delta fashion, were made from long gourds with narrow tops cut lengthwise, then seeded and dried. One was kept on the front porch for passersby; another, known as the "kitchen gourd," was used for cooking. Fieldhands knew they could find a cool drink of water in a tub with a gourd dipper which they all passed around.

Food on the farm went directly from the yard to the table. The cuisine was simple, but the plainness of some dishes was offset by their colorful, personalized names. "Stark Naked Rascus" was a batter boiled in water or stock and then enlivened with a syrup made of sugar and sweet spices. "Stocking-foot Molly" was a sticker made of flour batter.

"Nigger in the Blanket" was a fried pie filled with dried green peaches.

Farming was the family occupation. As each brother left home and married, he sharecropped or worked in the lumber industry until he could buy his own farm. Ivan did both. At the age of seventeen, he began working as a block-setter in a sawmill owned by J. L. Chives. Until automation made hand block-setting obsolete, Ivan worked in the mill during the summer and winter and farmed fall and spring. "The only sawmill work I ever done was settin' blocks," he says. But in 1964 he started a sawmill of his own to make railroad crossties; he sold it at a profit six years later when he retired.

Children's Games _____

Linda: Dad, tell 'em how you used to make string games.

Ivan: Oh, yeah. I used to teach Linda how we made things on a string...
looped string. I made one called "Crow's Foot." I made another'n called "Jacob's Ladder." I made another'n called "Joseph in the Coffin," and "See Saw." We used to have an ol' "zoop button." Put a button on a string, have two ends, put your hands in the thing and "zoop, zoop, zoop," just like elastic. I used to teach Linda all of that stuff.

Deirdre: How did you learn it?

Ivan: From my older sisters and brothers.

Linda: Tell 'em about how you used to play dolls.

Ivan: Yeah, we used to play dolls, the boys would play with the girls. We had one ol' doll was named Nathaniel. And we had one we called Brother. Then another'n we called ol' MANabathing...he was about a man's age. And Brother, Nathaniel, and Sister. That was all the dolls' names. We played with them and made dresses for them. We had a heap of ol' Biggity Wops. We couldn't fix THEM up good. Just put ANYTHING on them. But ol' Manabathing, Brother, Nathaniel, and Sister, them was special; we kinda fixed them up pretty good. Them was SPECIAL.

Deirdre: What did they look like?

Ivan: I don't imagine they looked very good...now! [General laughter.] They was PRETTY then.

Linda: How did y'all make 'em?

Ivan: Well, some of 'em we had an ol' piece of cloth and a stick. We wrapped a string around that cloth and make him a head. I don't know if they had arms or not. I know we didn't for ol' Biggity Wops. But ol' Manabathing, he was about a young man. Brother, he was a schoolboy. Nathaniel...Nathaniel was the baby. And Nathaniel was a girl. [Raucous laughter. Pause.] A woman came to visit us once, and she had a baby named Nathaniel. And we didn't know if it was a girl or a boy. So we named our ol' playchillen Nathaniel. That boy died about a year ago, Nathaniel Chives.

*Note: A "zoop-button" is made by stringing two feet of thread through two holes of a button and tying the string at one end. The player pulls the string taut by looping the string around the back of his hands and spreading his arms outward to the side. A rhythmic inward-outward motion of the arms sets up a tension and release in the string. The pressure caused by the button against the moving string gives the sound, "zoop, zoop.")

Ivan Johnson's smokehouse holds a recently cured ham.

The mill notwithstanding, Ivan felt that farming was his main business. For cash crops he grew tobacco, cotton, corn, peanuts, and sorghum, what he calls "that way back stuff." By the time Linda was born in 1943, the farm produced only about two bales of cotton a season. In time Ivan abandoned cotton and other cash crops; he never raised tomatoes, the hallmark of modern Bradley County farms. Linda's childhood experience touched mainly on the truck patch and the kitchen garden. Large, heavy vegetables like corn, sweet potatoes, white potatoes, and beets grew in the truck patch away from the house. Onions, radishes, string beans, and English peas were harvested as needed from the kitchen garden by the back door. There, greens grew all year round: spinach, mustard greens, fall cabbage, turnips, collards, kale, tender greens, and spring greens. Flour, meal, shortening, salt, and spices were, until recently, the only purchases made at the grocery store. Lemma canned vegetables and Linda churned the butter. Ivan salted and smoked the meat. Occasionally he went hunting, but he loved to fish above all. "He would walk down to Moro Creek," Linda says, "and fish all day long. If he caught two he would fish all day; if he caught a thousand he would fish all day."

An Extended Family. Lemma Johnson never ventured into her husband's outdoor domain of creeks, woodlands, and farm. Her realm was the kitchen ... or more properly two ... one her own and the other belonging to her employer Mrs. Claudia MacFarland. "Mr. Curtis" MacFarland owned the general mercantile store in Banks. For over

112

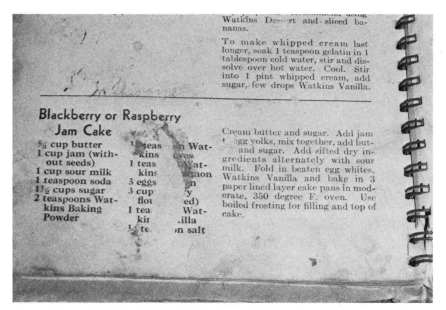

Watkins Dessert and sliced bananas.

To make whipped cream last longer, soak 1 teaspoon gelatin in 1 tablespoon cold water, stir and dissolve over hot water. Cool. Stir into 1 pint whipped cream, add sugar, few drops Watkins Vanilla.

Blackberry or Raspberry Jam Cake

⅔ cup butter
1 cup jam (without seeds)
1 cup sour milk
1 teaspoon soda
1⅓ cups sugar
2 teaspoons Watkins Baking Powder

1 teas   n Wat-
 kins   ⋯ves
1 teas   ⋯at-
 kin⋯   ⋯non
3 eggs   ⋯n
3 cup   ⋯y
 flo⋯   ⋯ed)
1 tea⋯   Wat-
 kir   .illa
¼ te   ⋯n salt

Cream butter and sugar. Add jam ⋯ egg yolks, mix together, add butter and sugar. Add sifted dry ingredients alternately with sour milk. Fold in beaten egg whites, Watkins Vanilla and bake in 3 paper lined layer cake pans in moderate, 350 degree F. oven. Use boiled frosting for filling and top of cake.

Lemma Johnson's famous recipe for Jam Cake.

twenty years Lemma labored over Miss Claudia's noon meal and came home when the dishes were done, around two o'clock.

It is generally agreed that Lemma was a woman of exceptional character. She came from a large family in Marsden, and when her mother Florence Texas Hines divorced, she was put in the charge of her mother's sister Jane. In time Lemma came to call her mother "Aunt Texas" and her aunt "Mother;" the Johnson children extended the titles to "Auntie" and "Grandma."

Mr. Curtis always drove Lemma home. Because of the way things were then, black folks in Banks knew a person needed a patron if they were going to get along, and Mr. Curtis was always reliable. The Johnsons could count on him to advance merchandise from his store; he was generous with references; and he lent people money to meet payments for loans. These deeds earned him the title "Bureau of Negro Affairs" from the younger generation.

If MacFarland was to the Johnsons an exceptionally good "patron," the Johnsons were to him very special "clients" indeed. "Family" is the word the Johnsons use to describe their relationship with their white employers, and it was true that in the person of Lemma the two families in some measure converged. She channelled stories, food traditions, customs, and clothing back and forth between the two halves of a unit that appeared as legitimate to its participants as any "family" in the extended or non-biological sense. Linda is sincere when she asserts, "Miss Claudia was like family to me, and my mother was like family to her son. But," she qualified, "of course the children were not like family to each other." The family extension took place at the level of elders and chiefly between Claudia and Lemma; for, in a certain way they were deep friends and never felt discomfort, for example, in shedding their patron-client roles to do Saturday shopping together. Youngsters, on the other hand, were participants through vertical relationships with older folks, not through horizontal relationships with peers.

Now that Claudia, and then Lemma, have passed on, the "extended family" tradition still survives in an echo of one of the many rituals enacted long ago. The MacFarland favorite among Mary's culinary triumphs was a pineapple cake, yellow with pineapple spread between the layers and seven-minute frosting that covered the sides and top. In her day the cake passed from her hands to their table on command, and underneath the cries of lavish praise that always met her production was the tacit understanding that, as a client, she could not easily refuse their request. Even so, the cake became a symbol for the ongoing affection between the two families. Whenever Linda visits her family in Banks, she finds time to make the pineapple cake for Gary, the MacFarland son. As an outright gift, today's gesture casts the extended family relationship into a different light. In a single generation Linda has become the patron, and in offering the cake the imbalance of past roles has symbolically been put right.

Celebrations, With And Without A Hitch. The new twist on the old pineapple cake ceremony is a sign of changing times. Today, life for the Johnson children holds opportunities their parents never knew. These new choices have also scattered them. Only sons Roy Lee and Wadell have stayed at home with Ivan in Banks. Eddie Ivan is a meatpacker in Los Angeles, where he forms a sub-family with sister Ola Mae. Ardell, Wadell's twin brother, is a barber in Jacksonville, and he is "family" to Linda, who teaches in the Alexander Youth Services Center near Little Rock, where she lives. By virtue of frequent trips to the homeplace, Linda maintains a link between the two Arkansas groups, and her "huge phone bill" to California proves her close ties with her older sister Ola Mae.

With urging from the older folks, the youngsters still take part in the periodic rituals that celebrate and acknowledge the kinship between members of the Johnson clan. A family reunion held in 1981 on the Fourth of July called Henry Johnson's descendants from Chicago, Detroit, Wisconsin, California, and Little Rock. Johnson homes in Banks and Warren strained to accommodate the twenty-five adults and their families; relatives "who would not have known each other on the street," as Linda put it, spent two days getting acquainted and participating in a program organized by a preacher in the family. At the church on Saturday night older folks made speeches and the preacher traced his family genealogy back to the times of slavery. Next day was an open-air picnic, where Ivan was photographed with his brother Lee Roy and their two oldest cousins. "It seems that picture would have had a thousand years on it," remarked Linda. "They're all so old!"

Another celebration that Linda remembers, however, has become a comic legend; it concerns the "hitches in getting hitched." Her marriage to Wilson Tolefree took place a few days before he was shipped out to Vietnam. It was a tense moment, but today Linda's twin daughters squeal with delight over the litany of mishaps they have by now learned by heart. "I wanted to do everything by the book," she laments, "but oh, that wedding was one...whee! It got off to a bad start..." and so the story begins. The car: "The day before we were married, my brother-in-law-to-be wrecked my car. So, we didn't have a car to go on our honeymoon." The cake: For last-minute errands at the florist's and bakery, they rented a vehicle, "but the cake was upset between his house and my home." The ring: "My mother had told me to slit the finger of my glove so

Courtship Stories ⎯⎯⎯⎯⎯⎯⎯⎯⎯⎯

Ivan: Three score and ten is the life of a man, but [on May 11, 1981] I'll be three score and twenty. I lived with my first wife...the only wife I had or ever will have...51 years, 5 months, and 11 days.

Deirdre: How did you meet your wife?

Ivan: Well, I was down in the little bitty town workin', and I would see her pass, goin' back and forth. So, I got to goin' and callin' on her. She was stayin' at her parents'. When I married, I was 24 and she was 19. We just went to the J.P. My family didn't know I'd got married 'til I brought her in there. The license was three dollars and the J.P. two dollars and a half. I went farming on the half the next year 'cause I wanted to be close to my wife. I didn't have nothin'...just the woman,...that's all I had. First year we got married, workin' on the half, I made six bales of cotton...picked it by myself.

Deirdre: How did you meet your husband Wilson?

Linda: It was in August or September, 1962. Anyway, I was getting ready to go off to college [Philander Smith]. He was a big-time sophomore [at UAPB]. So my friend saw him and his brother going up to the store. She had a crush on his brother. So she said, "Let's go up to the store; they're going up there." And I said, "Yeah, okay, let's go up to the store." So, while Wilson's brother was talking to my friend, I decided to mosey over to the produce section. He had decided to do the same thing. So we both reached for the same apple. He told me I could take it, and I told him he could take it. So, we haggled about who would take the apple. [Hearty laugh.] And that was the beginning of a beautiful relationship. I didn't see him any more until '63, the summer of '63. And after that I didn't see him until '64. I went to visit my aunt during the summer...down in Warren. I was pushin' her baby down the highway. I saw this car pass with this red thing hangin' out. It was his red Banlon shirt he was wearing. And he shouted, "Stop the car! Stop the car!" And I shouted, "Stop the car! Stop the car!" So, they stopped the car, and he got out, and we talked for awhile. I think I saw him about two more times before we got married, over a period of five years.

We still have that shirt, by the way. It doesn't have a single button on it, and it's all jacked up in the back. But we keep it.

115

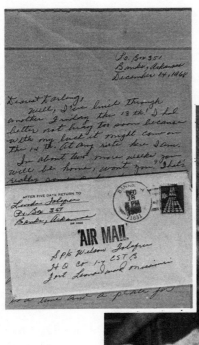

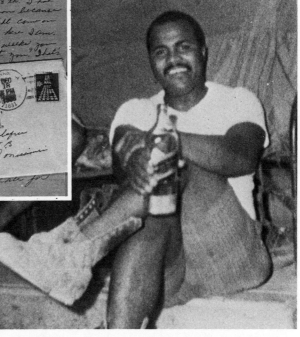

(Left) Wilson Tolefree has kept the letters his wife sent to Vietnam. (Below) Linda's favorite wartime photograph.

I could get my ring on without any hassle." She forgot, and when tugs gave way to yanks, "my bouquet flew to the ceiling and everyone thought I was tossing it!" Wilson's ring: Her brother-in-law left it behind in Warren, and when Mrs. Johnson's ring was presented as a substitute, "it wouldn't even go on his little finger!" Her daughter Kelly urged, "Tell about the rice." "My mother dyed rice and put it in bags, and my brothers-in-law started tossing them like baseballs. Whammo! Whammo!" And so, a mock battle brought the upside-down wedding to an end.

The tradition continues. Tales, customs and beliefs are nurtured and refurbished as they pass from one generation to the next. They bear witness to a family memory that draws upon tradition and at the same time safeguards it as the touchstone for the family's sense of purpose and self-worth. Family tradition is a never-ending source of "hogs in the bottom;" it replenishes its re-creators while they, in turn, complete the cycle by re-making, and thereby renewing, a sense of family lore.

—Deirdre LaPin

Family Tree

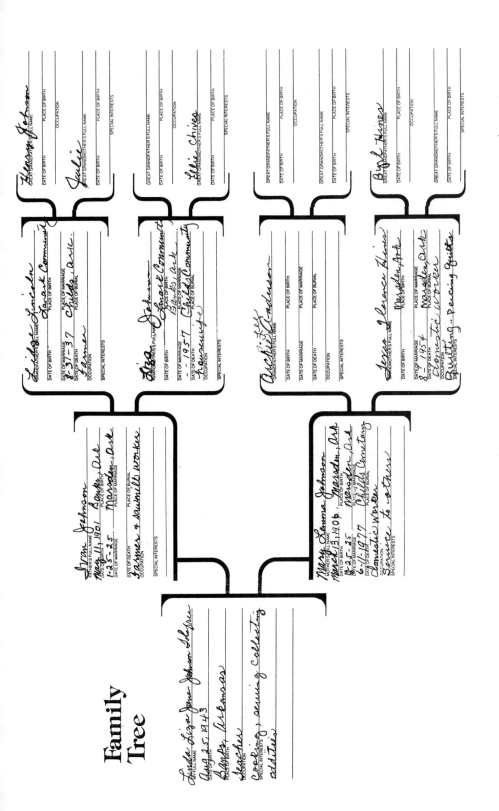

FULL NAME Linda Liza Jane Johnson Shaw
DATE OF BIRTH Aug 25, 1943
PLACE OF BIRTH Bigelow, Arkansas
OCCUPATION teacher
SPECIAL INTERESTS cooking, sewing, collecting antiques

FATHER'S FULL NAME Irvin Johnson
DATE OF BIRTH March 11, 1901 **PLACE OF BIRTH** Bon,e, Ark. **PLACE OF MARRIAGE** Marsden, Ark.
DATE OF DEATH 1-25-75
OCCUPATION farmer + sawmills worker
DATE OF BURIAL
SPECIAL INTERESTS

MOTHER'S FULL NAME Mary Lemma Johnson
DATE OF BIRTH March 3, 1906 **PLACE OF BIRTH** Marsden, Ark. **PLACE OF MARRIAGE** Marsden, Ark.
DATE OF DEATH 6-11-1977 **PLACE OF BURIAL** Childs Cemetery
OCCUPATION Domestic worker
SPECIAL INTERESTS Service to others

GRANDFATHER'S FULL NAME Luther Lincoln
DATE OF BIRTH **PLACE OF BIRTH** Sarark Community
DATE OF MARRIAGE 8-31-37 **PLACE OF MARRIAGE** Chivers, Ark.
DATE OF DEATH **PLACE OF BURIAL** Flemen
OCCUPATION
SPECIAL INTERESTS

GRANDMOTHER'S FULL NAME Ira Johnson
DATE OF BIRTH **PLACE OF BIRTH** Somere Community Bonle, Ark
DATE OF MARRIAGE **PLACE OF MARRIAGE**
DATE OF DEATH -- 1957 **PLACE OF BURIAL** Childs Community
OCCUPATION housewife
SPECIAL INTERESTS

GRANDFATHER'S FULL NAME Archie Anderson
DATE OF BIRTH **PLACE OF BIRTH**
DATE OF MARRIAGE **PLACE OF MARRIAGE**
DATE OF DEATH **PLACE OF BURIAL**
OCCUPATION
SPECIAL INTERESTS

GRANDMOTHER'S FULL NAME Jessie Glenese Hines
DATE OF BIRTH **PLACE OF BIRTH** Marsden, Ark.
DATE OF MARRIAGE 8--1954 **PLACE OF MARRIAGE** Marsden, Ark.
DATE OF DEATH **PLACE OF BURIAL**
OCCUPATION Domestic worker
SPECIAL INTERESTS Quilting - piecing quilts

GREAT GRANDFATHER'S FULL NAME Henry Johnson
DATE OF BIRTH **OCCUPATION**
PLACE OF BIRTH

GREAT GRANDMOTHER'S FULL NAME Julie
DATE OF BIRTH **OCCUPATION**
PLACE OF BIRTH **SPECIAL INTERESTS**

GREAT GRANDFATHER'S FULL NAME
DATE OF BIRTH **OCCUPATION**
PLACE OF BIRTH

GREAT GRANDMOTHER'S FULL NAME Ellie Chivers
DATE OF BIRTH **OCCUPATION**
PLACE OF BIRTH **SPECIAL INTERESTS**

GREAT GRANDFATHER'S FULL NAME
DATE OF BIRTH **OCCUPATION**
PLACE OF BIRTH

GREAT GRANDMOTHER'S FULL NAME
DATE OF BIRTH **OCCUPATION**
PLACE OF BIRTH **SPECIAL INTERESTS**

GREAT GRANDFATHER'S FULL NAME Bill Hines
DATE OF BIRTH **OCCUPATION**
PLACE OF BIRTH

GREAT GRANDMOTHER'S FULL NAME
DATE OF BIRTH **OCCUPATION**
PLACE OF BIRTH **SPECIAL INTERESTS**

Sadie (Callaway) Owens: "I could pick four hundred pounds of cotton in one day."

The Hollins-Callaway Family
"Keep An Open Hand"

A visitor approaches Tarry, Arkansas, from the eastern edge of Pine Bluff by turning south on Highway 81 toward Star City.

In summer, a rolling carpet of grass lines both sides of the road. Distant trees, like marching soldiers, shade the perimeter from the burning Delta sun. Several hundred yards down a dusty laterite side road, a tired frame building with several dislodged planks and partially-boarded windows stands silently, a ghost of Tarry's gasoline station and general mercantile store. Further on four neat, white houses, perhaps a block apart, come into view. They are the well-kept, attractive homes of the Callaway sisters — Lucy, Sadie, Mildred, Luvella — and their families. One block down lives brother Willie Callaway and across the street cousin Lucy Rivers and her husband.

The Homeplace. Lucy Callaway's house was once the "home house" of the Callaway clan. Grandfather William Callaway, about whose origins little is known except that "white name of Callaway raised him" resided here with his wife Lucy. In these walls their son Eddie J. Callaway, Sr., saw his wife Lelea Hollins give birth to twenty-five children, including three sets of twins; fourteen lived beyond six years of age. Lucy remembers when her grandfather's house burned down "on this very spot" shortly before the Second World War. Only the smokehouse, the cottonwood tree, and the crape myrtle survived. Family history explains that in 1927 grandfather William Callaway mortgaged the forty-acre homeplace to a McGehee banker. Though a

119

E. J.'s grandparents William and Lucy Callaway captured in retouched camera portraits.

responsible man, William was obliged to spend his meagre earnings on the repeated jail fines of his second, "bootleggin'" wife. Because of her shortcomings, the banker foreclosed. "Every time I looked around," says their eldest son Eddie J. Callaway, Jr., "[my parents] were moving from plantation to plantation. I resented the fact that my mother had to run from one job to another."

The younger Eddie ("E. J.") now owns a real estate business in the capital city. As a child he felt the seven-and-a-half-foot cotton sack fatten and heave against his small frame. It taught him a single-minded persistence that advanced him from sharecropping to domestic service in Little Rock, to the United States Army Cooking School, to Dunbar High School, to Philander Smith College, and finally to private enterprise.

In his own view, E. J.'s success is firmly grounded in his family upbringing. What his parents could not provide in material comfort, they furnished in sound training about the value of work, the importance of good character, and the nature of men and women in an unequal world. Proof of this legacy are the reminiscences about parents, who are best remembered for the lessons they taught. Their philosophy — a bulwark against disappointment, injustice, and financial duress — was rooted in the conviction that every person was indeed his brother's keeper. For them, society was more than a collection of individuals; it was an organism vitalized by human exchange. E. J.'s father put it this

E. J. Callaway presents a hanging portrait of his father Eddie J. Callaway, Sr., and his wife, Lelea (Hollins) Callaway.

way: "If you keep a closed hand, nothing will come in. If you have an open hand, you give and receive."

The fruit of their son's effort, borne of their own wisdom, nurtured the Callaway parents in ways that enriched the giver and receiver equally. While in the service during World War II, E. J. remembered his parents' lost homeplace and with the assistance of a Red Cross lawyer persuaded the banker to release the property for $1600. Eddie and Lelea, then sharecropping on "Mrs. Tower's place," moved back to the family land. "Papa had four mules and a wagon cleared with Mrs. Tower," E. J. recalls. "He never did tell her he was leavin' her place 'cause when he DID leave, she tol' him he done took her four best mules." A pre-fabricated "Jap" house was moved from a nearby detention center to the home site, and over the years E. J. has added nine rooms to the original four. In his will E. J. has included the condition that "as long as there is a Callaway, the house can never be mortgaged."

Lucy keeps a room in the home house for E. J. It contains their father's chair, family photographs, their mother's twin beds, and other keepsakes. Symbolically, the room binds E. J. to his family by assigning him a place at the geographical and historical center of the family compound. Inside the borders of the original "forty," the home house is flanked by the homes of his three sisters. The arrangement, which properly includes Willie down the road, is a structural expression of the blood ties that knit the members of the kin group; they are ties which would themselves be difficult to separate from the symbolic bond that joins the family collectively to the land. By his own admission, E. J. remains a "son of the soil." He returns to Tarry at least two weekends a month "to relax and enjoy the solitude and fresh, pure air." After his wife died in 1970 he turned to farming for solace, and during nearly four years thereafter made Tarry his home.

Since his father's death, the family has added to E. J.'s roles of landlord and eldest son that of the family patriarch. The part complements the matriarchal role that Lucy has played since her mother passed away (see p. 120). E. J. oversees the family's financial interests and maintains the farm and homes; Lucy presides over family holiday gatherings and puts up much of the family's food. On Mother's Day her siblings, children, and grandchildren lavish her with gifts, "so many," she says, "that I can't open them all." Lucy also maintains contact with siblings and relatives living nearby or far away; through her the central family at Tarry reaches its branch members: Reola in Yorktown and Leona in Sneed, Myrtle Lee in Kansas City, William in Los Angeles, Nathaniel and Theotus in Flint, Michigan; brother A. C. and sister Georgia also lived in Flint until their deaths not long ago. "If someone far away needs help," says Lucy, "we throw in a donation. And if another one needs help nearby, we do the same."

In the way of every homeplace, the life of the Callaway compound is a reflection of its history, and in several ways the roles that E. J. and Lucy play bring them into direct conjunction with the past. Lucy's namesake, her paternal great-grandmother "Lou," was such a well-loved family figure that her daughter "Lucy" had three children who in turn named daughters "Lucy" after her. E. J.'s predecessor in the role of patriarch was a more awesome figure in the person of step-great-grandfather Ishmael ("Ish") King. A man remembered for his almost mythical vitality, he was "125 years old" when he died in 1934. It is said that his eye-sight was so perfect that on any clear night "he could see the stars fall." Ish was not in fact a blood relation to the Callaway children, but the father of grandmother Georgia's second husband, Hayward King. Georgia left her first husband, West Hollins, behind in Bastrop, Louisiana, when she and her young daughter Lelea moved north. Old Man King exercised an authority the family rarely challenged. When, for example, he named baby sister Sadie "Ishmael" for himself, her mother Lelea dutifully recorded it on her birth certificate, although the name was never used. No one recalls where Ish was born, where he lived in his younger years, or whether Emancipation changed his life. But it is certain that, like the Callaways, he was a sharecropper in the Tarry cottonfields during the second half of the last century. Perhaps he found so little difference between sharecropping and slavery, its parent institution, that he never perceived the transition worthy material for passing on in stories to his step-grandchildren.

Plantation Life. When he thinks about life on the plantation, E. J. vows with brutal candor, "I really learned how to deal with people because you had to in order to survive back in those days. The plantation was the most sickening thing you ever saw in your life; anybody who lived on a plantation, they can tell you." A day in the Callaway household began at four o'clock. Lelea rose and prepared a large breakfast, usually of oatmeal and side pork, and she also packed a lunch bucket if the day's work was too distant for a noon meal at home. In the dim light of the pre-dawn, she thrust the bucket into waiting hands, and the little band of laborers set off for the fields down the rutted dirt road. Lessons were taught in mid-winter and summer seasons, and Lelea believed firmly in the training that took place in the two-room schoolhouse. Classes combined several grades, one through five and six through eleven. But at planting and chopping time, the older children followed their elders to the farm, and with a certain pride they measured their progress in pounds of unginned cotton: from under a hundred for the youngsters to well over three hundred for adults.

During her child-bearing years, Lelea and a daughter or two would generally stay home to tend babies and cook the family's meals. But, like

---

Home Remedies

Plantation doctors in Tarry were few, and transportation was rarely available. Added to the many roles mothers played was keeping their families healthy. Home remedies were handed down from mother to daughter or passed on from other relatives and friends. Almost any mother was certain to have a mental list of cures for the most common ailments and accidents.

Colds:

Dip a piece of yarn into melted beef tallow; place over chest and secure with two safety pins. "That will draw it right out."

Onion tea. Heat onions and sugar with tallow, water, and whiskey. Drink very hot.

Cedar tea. Take "regular plain old cedar" and boil it to make a bitter tea that "cleans you right out for the winter."

Three six's (666), a patent medicine.

Cleaning Out:

Black Draught.

Cuts:

Wash with Epsom salts.

Apply salt and smut, wrap it well. In a day or two wash with water and clean with peroxide.

Splinters:

Put fat salt meat on a splinter, briar, or glass. "It draws it to a head."

Teeth:

For tooth aches, use a strong lemon rub.

Clean teeth by brushing on salt and soda, using a chewing stick split from a snuff box or a tree. "We didn't buy toothbrushes or anything like that."

For "pretty, white teeth" rub well with a rag and baking soda.

her children, she was inured to hard, physical labor. She told her children about the times she cleared the "new ground," undeveloped bottomland, on the plantation. During the weeks when all hands were urgently needed, she too joined the field hands. Her daughter Sadie Owens recalls the change as a welcome escape from the domestic routine: "I used to cry about staying home. Mama said, 'I'm going to put you in the fields to work.' And so at that time they had a seven-and-a-half-foot cotton sack and a nine-foot cotton sack. But she gave me a seven-foot sack, and she tol' me, 'I'm going to take up your strap and I'm going to give you one row and put you around the side of me.' And oh, I'd get my one row and I'd pick cotton, and then I'd pick off of HER row. And so I was pickin' so much off HER row, she give me TWO rows [laughter]. That made it WORSE. I had to pick HARD to keep up! So, every now and then they'd help me with my two rows, and I would PICK COTTON, HEAR?" Later, when she was grown, Sadie would pick four hundred pounds a day.

Raising cotton was a hard living, but in Tarry "work" and "cotton" were one and the same. Even recently, before the local farms were fully mechanized, Sadie could substantially improve her income by taking leave from her domestic job in October and working the harvest until Christmas time. Understandably, the business-minded E. J. now judges sharecropping a system filled with abuses. "It was ridiculous the way people did people in those days," he remarks. "You'd get to the field before sun-up. When we finished chopping our crop, we'd chop for the day, get fifty cents a day." His parents worked on "the half," meaning that they divided the selling price of their crop equally with the landowner. From the family's share, the owner subtracted fees for equipment and tools, mules and feed, and credit advanced at the plantation store. A small income could be made during the picking season on the "seed money" earned on the seed ginned from the cotton at the end of every week. During the season a family could nearly live on the amount, but season's end often proved the sharecropping system unfair: "When you'd picked about one half of your field, "the Man" would ask how much you had left [to pick] so you'd get just enough [profit] to buy your food. You weren't there to sell your cotton; he told you what he'd sell your cotton for. You got one price and he got a higher one in Pine Bluff. And at the end of the last three or four bales, he'd add your debts up and tell you how much you owed. Maybe you cleared two hundred dollars for the whole year. So, what could you do? Simply go to the next plantation and maybe do a little better."

In the face of hardship Lelea was a good manager. She kept the family accounts unerringly in her head. She taught the girls to knit, quilt, and crochet in leisure hours and expected her boys to know how to cook. She sent the family to church on Sunday morning and to the Baptist Training Union ("BTU") every week. Her children were organized into a disciplined working unit, and when their work away from home was finished, they returned to duties she assigned. Washing for the large family, Lucy recalls, was a notably heavy chore: "We would wash every day, come home from the fields and from work and set out tubs outside under that ol' hickory tree, and they'd be two of us washin' and two of us wrenchin' and hangin' out. We turn them lights on and we would wash at night and get our clothes the next mawnin' by moonshine light."

Today the Callaways hint at the urgency of survival that possessed their mother who had lost nine children through accident, disease, and overwork. She gave birth to three sets of twins who died in early childhood. However common death may have been, it was never met with resignation. Eddie vividly recalls the sad tale of a two-year-old brother who died from pneumonia after falling from a plank bridge into ditchwater below. Lelea believed that stern discipline was one way of keeping her children from harm, and family stories often portray her as a swift and uncompromising enforcer of domestic rules. Children were expected to sit quietly in the presence of adults and to never look at them directly when they spoke. Outdoor play was bound by the admonition, "Don't let sundown catch you away from home" (see "Proverbs And Sayings: Family Wisdom," p.126). Any grown boy returning home after midnight found the doors and windows boarded and had to make his bed in the fields. E. J. remembers a tale about a sound thrashing he, his sister and cousins received for ignoring their mother's interdiction about eating unripe muscadines: "We had a muscadine tree out there in the woods, and mother always tol' us to wait until the muscadines got ripe. And so Mama went somewhere one day — I think she went over to Tarry to do some shoppin' — and this lady saw us out there by the muscadine tree, and she told Mama about it, and she came home to my cousin and myself and my older sister Lucy. And you talk about somebody whopped somebody 'bout those muscadines! I think that was one of the best whoppin's I ever seen in my life!"

Lelea's obvious concern about her children's welfare lent weight to her repeated assertion, "I'm whippin' you because I LOVES you." She loved the family enough to keep it working harmoniously as a unit; she also loved her children enough to keep them on good terms with powerful strangers. "She wanted people to love her children," says Lucy, "so that people would do favors when they asked...I loves to get along with people." Good behavior, in Lelea's view, was a skill learned chiefly for survival.

"Growin' A-Plenty And Puttin' Up A-Plenty." E. J. is grateful that, while the family did not wear fine clothes or have a fine house, its members never wanted for food. The variety of vegetables produced in the garden could be judged from the greens alone: turnip tops, kale, mustard greens, beet tops, collards, poke sallet, and occasionally spinach. For meat and eggs Lelea raised ducks, geese, chickens, turkeys, and guineas. Fruit from apple, pear, peach, plum, and persimmon trees found their way into pies and jams. A large part of the food was preserved for winter. "We did it then just like I am today," Lucy said on a day in June. "I canned yesterday. I canned chow chow, I canned jelly, I put up string beans." In November Eddie J., Sr., would slaughter hogs and smoke the meat with hickory chips, while Lelea canned or pickled the beef. "We'd have meat," Lucy declared, "'til meat time again."

Hunting and fishing were popular sports among the Callaway brothers, and the fresh catch was a common addition to the family table. Minks, coons, opposums, and other small fur-bearing animals were an additional source of revenue for the rural farmer. Meanwhile, on rainy days when the fields were too wet for work, the girls descended into the woods to collect "scalabars," hickory nuts, and walnuts. Dried and hulled, they were packed into barrels along with homegrown peanuts, popcorn, and rivencams and set in the smokehouse for wintertime snacks.

The tradition that Lucy names "growin' a-plenty and puttin' up a-plenty" is still maintained through family co-operation. Sadie's large

Proverbs And Sayings: Family Wisdom

Proberbs, observed Kenneth Burke, are "strategies for living." Received out of the past, their economy of words belies the rich accumulation of human experience from which they are distilled. Timeless, abstract, stripped to the core, they project solutions onto future situations by observing them from specific vantage points. One person faced with a difficult task may tackle it slowly, believing that "Haste makes waste," while another may jump in without delay because "He who hesitates is lost."

In families, proverbs and sayings are an oral inheritance that represent the strategies and attitudes most valued by remembered ancestors. Some are personal responses to certain problems their ancestors experienced in their own lives; others are direct charges to their descendants. Strong commands, uttered in strong, poetic language, they are easily recalled and frequently recited. The children of Eddie and Lelea Callaway often portray their parents as propounders of proverbial warnings, admonitions, and reminders. Each belongs to a context bearing upon a specific facet of their lives: business, interpersonal relations, family discipline. Proverbs enshrine past solutions as models for the present, where they are accepted and acted upon as the legacy of former generations.

A point of character:

My Daddy used to tell us, "If you have a closed hand, nothing will come in; if you have an open hand, you give and receive. *Keep an open hand*."

(Eddie J. Callaway, Jr.)

A point of ethics:

We had a real good mother. She tried to teach us right. She say, "Whatever you do, I want you to work for your living. That what we does. We works, we works for a living. *The honest way is the best way*."

(Lucy Harris)

A guide to business:

My Daddy always said, *"Learn a person and watch the pennies. If you make a dollar, save a quarter, always. Never put all your eggs in one basket; scatter them."* Now that has been my tradition.

(Eddie J. Callaway, Jr.)

A point of faith:

Before my mother died, she tole me, she say, "Lucy — she asked me three times — would you take care of those kids at the house there, and see after 'em and raise 'em until they gets big enough to do for theirselves. Now listen what Mama wants you to do; Mama wants you to make them work like I did ya'll." And she said, "Whatever you do, give my children a-plenty to eat. And put clothes on them. And don't worry how you're going to make it with them because *the Lord always has a way out."* I give my answer, and she say, "Well, Mama got the word and Mama satisfied."

(Lucy Harris)

A succour:

I remember when my wife, who has no sisters or brothers, was sick in the hospital and needed clean robes, gowns, and things. I took the clean things to her in the hospital and picked up the soiled pieces and laundered them for her. It was then I thought about what my mother and grandmother had said, *"You can learn it. If you have to do it, you will know HOW to do it."*

(Eddie J. Callaway, Jr.)

A point of discipline:

In the future life we had a great mother, but when we was comin' up, I thought she was a mean mother. Our Mama used to tell us, *"Don't let sundown catch you 'way from home."* That evenin' we got to playin' so and the sun was a-comin', you know, behind the tree. So we ran, we ran, we ran. We met our mother with a long stick, and my Auntie was with her. We met her with this long switch. We met her, she say, "I tole y'all not to let the sun catch you down." We say [in a high tone] "Mama, we didn't... we overplay oursel..." And so, Auntie was with her, and she begged, "Don't whip 'em this time. The sun is just over behind the trees. Don't whip 'em this time."

So my Auntie say, "Lucy, don't you see that skeeta on your leg?" I said, "No 'em." She say, "That skeeta been on you leg ever since we met you." She say, "You didn't...?" I said, "No 'em. I was lookin' over there at that switch she had!" [Laughter].

(Lucy Harris)

A rule for living:

Lois: From your parents, what traditions have you learned that helped you most in life?

Eddie: Shortly before my mother died she said, *"Help people get where you are."* I have been trying. My motto is, "Serve Humanity" because at one time other people helped me and made me so happy.

(Eddie J. Callaway, Jr.)

A bawdy saying:

One time, I was walkin' through the house, and I was sayin' *"Ole cat like cheese like a young cat like cheese."* My mama took a broom and said, "Where you get that word from?" I heard my grandma sayin' that.

(Eddie J. Callaway, Jr.)

Kitchen in the Callaway home, dating from the time of grandmother. Says Lucy (Callaway) Harris: "She canned back then just like I do today."

truck patch supplies the family with vegetables, and the surplus is sold in town. Lucy raises a few chickens and hogs and cans Sadie's vegetables. A nephew who works in a nearby meat-packing house keeps Lucy's freezer filled at wholesale prices. E. J. brings food scraps to Lucy's hogs and, completing the cycle, rarely returns home without fresh vegetables or a jar of chow chow.

Holidays and funerals are the chief occasions for family reunions at the home place. In September, 1980, brother A. C. Callaway was buried in Tarry. "I slept and fed forty right here at this house," Lucy recalls, "and I fed more because a lot of them stayed up at the motel." Anticipating the large numbers, she expanded her store of canned vegetables, ham, and beef with sixty pounds of chicken, sixty pounds of ribs, twenty dozen eggs, and six gallons of milk. "Nobody had to go to the store." For three days the family was fed in shifts: breakfast at six, eight, ten, and twelve o'clock, dinner at one and three; and light snacks for dinner.

Lucy, who "cooks by feel, not by recipes" takes pride in re-creating her mother's desserts: gingerbread, tea cakes, butter rolls, buttermilk pie, white bean pie, Irish potato pie, sweet potato pie, custard pie, and grandmother Hollins' pound cake. At Christmas dinner jam cake, carrot cake, lemon pies, and coconut pies are standard fare. They are served — along with turkey, ham, barbecued ribs, potato salad, cranberries, and assorted vegetables — buffet-style to nearly seventy people. Christmas dinner and a gift exchange is all that remains of the childhood holiday,

Prosperity gives the old homeplace a new look.

when white stockings were hung at the fireplace and stuffed with nuts, apples, oranges, and a quarter in the toe. The reason, Lucy and Sadie make plain, is that their jobs as domestic workers have put them in holiday service to other families. Indeed, as a family celebration, Christmas has survived in large measure because the day also marks Lucy's birthday.

Food, as the chief focus of a sharecropper's life, meant both pleasure and security to the Callaway family. For E. J., Lelea's cooking lessons became the stepping-stone from plantation to city living. At the age of twenty he took a job as a domestic cook with a Little Rock car dealer and former county judge. While attending high school in the morning, he earned $1.50 a week plus room and board for doing afternoon chores. "On Sundays," he recalls, "I used to fix those big dinners and get an extra dollar when all the children came in every other week. I was really proud of that." On joining the army in World War II he was trained in baker's school and was soon promoted from first cook to mess sergeant. After the War he worked briefly as a fry cook at the Albert Pike Hotel and later as a cook at Fort Roots. In retrospect, he observes, "That good training my mother and grandmother instilled in me helped me in the army."

From the judge, his first employer, Callaway also learned the business of real estate. "He'd buy houses, and I'd fix them up." Later, he would confess that he made his living in the business chiefly because it brought a high profit. Cooking was his passion and remains a permanent hobby. "Lord," he cries emphatically, "I LOVE to COOK!" Pies are his strong point, in keeping with the family tradition, and he packs them by the dozen into his large freezer. When his children come by, they reportedly ask, "Do you have a pie in there, Daddy?"

Home house, stories, sayings, names, and food traditions still permeate every facet of the Arkansas Callaways' lives. Bound up with the Delta bottomland, these family traditions bear witness to a former style of life. Because the family, like most men and women, welcome the familiarity of old habits and traditions, these folk images are still nurtured. Their special power is to shape future ideas and actions of tradition-bearers by supplying them with a firm grounding in the past. The proverb "keep an open hand," in the context of folk tradition, is more than an example of family wisdom; indeed, the act of transmitting wisdom is a clear application of its lesson. For wisdom, a gift of present to future generations, is amply repaid in the conviction that philosophical continuity within the family group will ensure the well-being of all its members.
                                                    —Lois Pattillo
                                                    Deirdre LaPin

Clear.

Make chart for Paternal Step Grandfather
Ish King, Hayward, Father, Father of Ish
125 yrs old King

Unknown

Calloway Genealogy Chart

1918 Edgie J. Calloway, Jr.
1919 Lucy ____ King

William
Georgia
Millie
Sadie
Luvella
Mildred
Theodis
N.C.
Reola
Leona
Myrtle Lee
Nathaniel

Eddie J. Calloway Jr.
Born ____ Died 1916

Married 1917

Lila Holine
Born 1903 Died 1962

William Calloway
Paternal Grandfather

Lucy Calloway
____ Grandmother

Hoet Holine
____ Grandfather

Georgia ____
____ Grandmother

Hayward King

Ismael King
Born 1808
Died 1934

Make place for
14 + boy
that died

| You and your Brothers + Sisters | Your Parents | Your Grandparents | Your Great Grandparents |

Everett Tucker, Jr., gazes at a portrait of his great-grandfather Charles Josephus Tucker (1800-1856). He traveled in a wagon train from Powhatan County, Virginia, to Falkville, Alabama, in the 1820s.

The Williams-Tucker Family
On The Edge Of The Delta

Voices from the C.B. radio pierced the still evening that was settling over central Arkansas. The man had stepped down from his white Chevrolet pick-up and now stood leaning, elbows akimbo, over the open door to gaze down the two-lane road. His eye studied the stand of soybeans framed against a haze of heat. About two miles behind, the green rice fields began and continued to the south and west where they filled almost five hundred of the nearly three thousand acres of Tucker family land. What the man, a renter on the Tucker place, saw most clearly was that something was missing. It saddened him a little. "There's great sentimentality about cotton," he offered. "Nobody drives by a one million dollar stand of soybeans and says, 'Oh, what a lovely stand of beans.' They could care less. It's just money. But a pitiful, scraggly mess of cotton is, 'Look at that cotton!'"

If the landowner and operator Everett Tucker, Jr. could indulge a wish, cotton would, on his plantation, still be "king." Today his land is subject to different rule. "Nobody makes money on cotton the way they used to." The renter's words summed up the hard truth. Long ago he, Mr. Tucker, and the other two farmers who rent the Tucker land had in their individual ways seen mechanization, synthetics, competition for labor, manufacturing and marketing costs undermine the place of cotton in Delta agriculture and with it the way of life that cotton had made.

Yet inside the families that comprise the "old planter aristocracy" (the phrase is "Tuck's"), cotton still underpins the identity which family members have collectively granted themselves. The sense of place that goes with the old cotton plantation historically anchors them — even their descendants who follow an urban way of life — in an old Arkansas tradition. If time has cast them out of the Delta, memories, lore, and historical record allow them to rest on its edge.

From Yankee Dollar A Plantation Doth Grow. Grandfather John Woodfin Tucker died before Tuck was born, but his grandson remembers hearing about how his Scottish ancestor journeyed from Powhatan County, Virginia, to Falkville, Alabama, in the 1820s. John's father, Charles Josephus Tucker, was a schoolteacher and a farmer, who "led a comfortable life but probably didn't live in Alabama long enough to accumulate a lot of land." A story fragment remains of his legendary love affair with Anne Obedience Drake. Contrary to her name, she married against her father's wishes and left with her husband shortly thereafter to seek a new home. Their wagon train probably included the Dinsmores and the Pattersons, who settled in Falkville and intermarried with a number of the twelve Tucker children until the families were scattered by the Civil War. John was only sixteen when he joined the Confederate Army as a drummer boy or bugler. "He may have seen combat," says Tuck modestly, "but I'm not sure."

What the Tuckers do remember and refer to repeatedly is that John is the hero of a rags-to-riches tale. "In 1866 or '67 he got off a steamboat in Pine Bluff with a silver dollar in his pocket," Tuck recounts. He went to work in a sawmill, bought 200 acres of Jefferson County land, built a sawmill, cleared the trees and sold lumber and became one of the county's large planters. "I remember the sawmill [started in 1888] was gone when I was a child, but there was a big ol' sawdust pile down there. They built the [new] cotton gin on the same spot where the sawmill had been."

Dual Traditions: Books And Tales, Fixed And Flux. The Tuckers are one of those families who, by virtue of property, longevity, politics, and wars are reference points in the general flow of human experience. Wholly private events that would elsewhere be lived and recounted by the family alone in their case become matters of public interest. Eventually the legends of these aristocrats pass out of oral tradition and come to rest in print. Consequently, the Tuckers, like prominent families before them, have entrusted historians with much of their past. For details about who they are and where they came from, the bookshelf is now an important source.

A dual tradition, then, carries the burden of Tucker family history. Ancestor stories, transmitted by word of mouth, reflect the perspectives of current users; written accounts, attending to detail and fact, are frozen in their times. Characteristically, the versions of events drawn from the two sources do not, when compared, always agree. For example, Goodspeed, who included biographies of notable citizens in his histories of Arkansas counties nearly a hundred years ago, painted his "Captain [John W.] Tucker" for an audience quite different from the Tuckers today. In an era when the hardships of pioneering were the common lot of many, the seemingly glorious asides of war experiences made more memorable copy. Goodspeed's "Captain Tucker" received praise as an incarnation of the old South. The chronicler wrote that John served in Company I, Fifth Alabama Cavalry, under General Forrest. Listing the battles in which he fought, Goodspeed concludes: "His record through the war is one that reflects the greatest credit on himself, for its heroic action in time of danger, and many times he has received the cheers of his comrades for performing some daring piece of work." Quite an elaboration on the limited and cautious account of grandfather's war experience given orally by Tuck.

Moreover, today's rags-to-riches tale shows that the family, despite the orthodoxy of print, has never relinquished the right to interpret history to fit its present needs. To them, the broad outline of events in John's life are cast into a recognizable "success" type that shapes a powerful charge to the current generation: Inheritors of John Tucker's effort, follow his example and with hard work preserve the financial legacy he left.

When John W. Tucker passed away suddenly on October 27, 1980, he left behind a Plum Bayou plantation of 2,800 acres. It included a general mercantile store, a sawmill, a ginning operation, schools for black and white children, a blacksmith and a carpenter's shop, four houses, fifty to sixty four-room sharecropper cabins, and a post office and Cotton Belt railway station both named "Tucker" after him. John's family had inherited a small fiefdom. Who would take charge? Of the five children who survived among the nine Sarah Eliza (Morrow) Tucker bore, a successor was not readily apparent. Oldest daughter Mary Edna McKnight had married Waddell A. McKnight of Cairo, Illinois; her

Hoppin' Tom
Tuck: We had this old colored man who was my mother's yardman. And he was paid $3.50 a week. And he milked the cows in the morning and again at night, did the dishes, cut the grass, and was just a great old character. But he had this talent, that if it had come along a little sooner we would have put him on T.V., and we could have all retired. And I don't know how he got this idea, but he took a wooden broomstick handle and put some double-jointed legs connected by a wire or something ... I don't believe he had arms ...

Francis: I think it did ...

Tuck: Maybe it did ... I guess it DID have arms ... and then ran a string through the hole where the head would have been and put the string over his knee and then he'd stand there and say: "Teemo Skitchet Hoppin' Tom. If he don' hop he don' get no corn." And he had other songs. And our generation would have him come down for a hayride and put him on, and they'd just EAT IT UP. He was the BEST entertainment they'd ever seen! And HE just ate it up, too!

(Above) Tucker, Arkansas. D. Everett
Tucker, Sr., holds "Junior" as his wife
Will Lynne and mother Sarah Eliza
look on. (Right) Cadet Tucker at
Sewanee Military Academy.

sister Bessie had moved to Charleston, Missouri, with her husband John
G. Russell. Charles Sidney was off to Oklahoma to seek his fortune and
his younger brother John W., Jr., was still a boy. Bachelor Uncle
("Ceph") Josephus had joined his brother during Reconstruction, but at
his age the task of managing a plantation was too great.

The lot fell to another brother, D. Everett, the middle of the three
sons. Assuming the role of "Captain" of Tucker Plantation was for him a
difficult choice. His father had sent him to study law at Washington and
Lee because the Confederate General Robert E. Lee had been president
of the school, and when he completed his legal studies in Little Rock, he
opened a law firm in Pine Bluff. Shortly after, he was elected to the lower
house of the State Legislature as Jefferson County Representative in
1906.

Tuck believes his father is one of the few Representatives in Arkansas history who resigned from the Legislature while holding office. His
commitment to the planter's life was sudden and complete. While his
legal education gained him stature among the county planters, he had to
learn the cotton business, not through training, but through resolve.
"Gramma" Sara Eliza Tucker and his younger brother John were immediately entrusted to his care. He took over management of the day
hands, maintenance crew and the riding bosses. But his greatest human
responsibility was the five dozen sharecropper families whose toil transformed the land into cotton and corn. Mules, plows, and hand tools had to
be supplied, along with food, medicine, clothing, and domestic needs
that were "furnished" on the first of every month. By March the share-

croppers' incomes from the previous harvest would have been spent, and most would live on credit from the Tucker store until August when picking began again. To offset his risk from default and the interest lost on his credit advance, Everett added twenty per cent to the regular cash purchase price of supplies. This was the customary practice at that time.

In addition to his other duties, Everett, Sr. was a director on the Tucker school board. About thirty-five children attended grades one through eight, including the Nivens, whose property adjoined the Tucker land to the east. Family photos show youngsters from the two plantations striking elegant poses at lawn parties in the Tucker back-yard. Other children came from the households of the warden at Tucker prison and the overseers on the Tucker and Niven land. Sharecroppers sent their children to another school that had a different curriculum and meeting schedule. Education was separate, but far from equal, as Tuck recounts in a story he frequently tells (see "How Do You Spell Constan-tinople?," pg. 141).

The Country Life. The Tucker family compound included a one-story house on the west side of the railroad, where Tuck, or "Junior" as he was called then, lived with his parents and sister. Across the track Gramma Tucker stayed in the large, two-story home that she and her husband built as a sequel to the original cypress structure that stood, abandoned, about two miles west on the bank of Plum Bayou. A great matriarch, she enjoyed a figurehead reign over the little colony, where her needs in queenly fashion were met on demand. Her household included a black companion and a cook; her Buick was driven by a part-time chauffeur; her food and domestic needs, including quinine (for malaria), were supplied by the plantation store; and her son was gener-ous with "spondoolix," her word for cash. She and her grandson "Junie" (Tuck) had a special relationship, and at breakfast she repaid his over-night visits with forbidden coffee and as much "spondoolix" as a boy in rural Tucker could use.

As a young man Tuck admits that just like his father in his youth, he "couldn't WAIT to get away from Tucker, Arkansas." The little town was isolated. It took one hour to reach Pine Bluff by car, two hours to travel thirty miles to Little Rock. Isolation was aggravated by long winters. "In wintertime, unless you had a month of dry weather, you didn't go anywhere by car, but you could take the train."

Tuck's well-rehearsed personal story follows a circular, and almost epic, design. It begins with his "escape" from the country to Sewanee Military Academy, continues through his schooling at Washington and Lee, covers his courtship of Francis Williams, follows his experiences of the Depression and Second World War, describes a bout with tuber-culosis, and comes to rest in Little Rock, not far (35 miles) from his Tucker Plantation home. The outline is filled with humorous detail in every scene; throughout the planter tradition is the chief point of reference.

Rather than return directly to lonely Tucker after graduation from college, Tuck took a job in 1934 at a Little Rock Standard Oil station as a "management trainee." He chuckles at the high-sounding title: "All I did was pump gas." The company leased all its stations in 1936, and he returned to the plantation, where his father gave him a '32 Chevrolet coupe and, it turned out, let him draw a sixty dollar monthly salary.

From this point it was Tuck's turn to master the plantation business. The gin was in full production: "We never ginned on Monday. On Tuesdays we got five to six bales, Wednesdays eight to ten; by Friday we usually had twenty-five to thirty. That was about the most for a week." The sharecroppers worked "on the halves," splitting the proceeds of the cotton 50-50. "In those days," he recalls, "the Negro sharecropper didn't WANT the responsibility for selling his crops, plus he wanted the money as quickly as he could get it." For an owner, sharecropper children were an asset. Land parcelled out to each family was calculated according to the number of children aged ten years and up. Besides sharecropping "we always had a day crop," Tuck adds, where laborers could earn seventy-five cents for a fourteen-hour day. The pay was low, but for a sharecropper, it was preferable to debt.

World War II interrupted Tuck's second life on the old plantation. After Pearl Harbor he enlisted in the U.S. Army Air Corps; he won a place at Harvard Business School as a part of his training as an officer candidate. "When they handed me a slide rule, I didn't even know what it was!" Commissioned in January, 1943, as a Second Lieutenant, he joined a group of Arkansas officers at Newcastle Army Air Base in Wilmington, Delaware. Under the command of Colonel Robert H. Baker from Little Rock, the little group seemed bent on matchmaking. Deputy Commander Joe Ledbetter and his wife Judy "encouraged" their friend Francis Williams to come visit Tuck, although "ostensibly she was staying with them." The couple, according to the groom, had been "going together for five or six years, not passionately or vigorously. They say Judy was eavesdropping at the top of the stairs when I popped the question." What prompted his wife's assent? "It was the uniform," Francis vows.

Little Rock Society. Tuck maintains with only partial seriousness that the match was foreshadowed by the sale of some land near Tucker. Three weeks before his death in 1908, John W. Tucker's last purchase was a track from the firm of Yowell and Williams, Francis' grandfather.

In every other way, the families were very different. Francis was, like her mother Marion, named after Francis Marion, the "Swamp Fox" (although she claims no blood relationship to him). She descended from urban dwellers whose lives focused on politics and society, not on agriculture. What the folklore of the two families does have in common, however, is the historical prominence and legendary reputation of the

Miss Francis Williams

Miss Williams, also a Vassar graduate, having received her degree this past June, is the daughter of Mr. and Mrs. Robert Monroe Williams. She's also the little girl with the doll buggy and the other was taken while out sailing when she visited last year in Rochester, N. Y., as the guest of Martina Callihan.

An old scrapbook filled with newspaper clippings, invitations, ribbons, photographs, and programs commemorates Francis (Williams) Tucker's graduation from Vassar and debut in 1936.

Senator James P. Clarke (to left under clock) presiding as president *pro tempore* of a joint session of Congress called to announce U.S. entry into World War I.

family patriarchs. Francis' grandfather James P. Clarke was both an Arkansas governor and three-term U.S. Senator. A photograph hanging prominently in the Tucker household shows Clarke as president *pro tempore* at the joint session of Congress where Woodrow Wilson made his declaration of war. Other photographs, now a tradition in the family, show various members standing next to the Senator's statue on view at the Capitol Building in Washington.

"Tempestuous," "obstreperous," "trickish" are adjectives published accounts attached to "old cotton top" Clarke. In oral tradition his adult life is marked by a series of legends. He was possessive of his daughters Julia and Marion, and he relished playing pranks on his sons-in-law. He was known to douse them with a water hose when they approached the family house at Thirteenth and Scott. One evening, Joe House, Julia's husband, chose not to enter the premises where the only light shone from upstairs. "The lights," he said punning, "were not on in the House; they were on in the Senate!" The Senator's daughter Marion (Clarke) Williams remembers when Woodrow Wilson visited her father's hotel room personally after the two men locked horns over the President's ship-purchase bill. It called for creating a federal corporation to purchase merchant ships for carrying American goods during the First World War. Clarke was so vehement in his opposition to the plan that "it kinda caused a commotion." It is recounted also that the statesman preserved his image to the end. Suffering a heart attack on September

Tucker Plantation established 1871.

How Do You Spell Constantinople?

Tuck: Something which could relate to my subsequent service on the Little Rock School Board [1959-1963] during integration was a conversation I had one day with a playmate.* The only kids we had to play with [on Tucker Plantation] were colored children. Of course, we had separate schools, and they had an entirely different curriculum. And I was reminded of this three years ago when Francis [his wife] and I made a trip over to Greece and Turkey, and we went on to Istanbul. I thought there was something familiar about it. I remembered afterward what that little girl told me she learned in school that day:

She said, "I'll tell you one thing I learned."

And I said, "What's that?"

And she said, "I learned how to spell 'Constantinople.'"

I said, "What?"

"That's a town over there."

And I said, "Well, how do you spell it?"

And she said, "A 'con' and a 'stan' and a 'con-stan-ti,' a "steeple' and a 'stople' and a 'con-stan-ti-no-ple.' That's the way you spell it."

I'm realistic enough to know that "separate but equal" was not equal. My father was on the school board at the time when segregation was legal, and they hired teachers who taught [black children] how to spell "Constantinople" instead of what they should have been teaching.

I've forgotten a lot of things, but I'll never forget that.

(*Note: Tuck was President of the Board during his tenure and in August, 1959, discussed the Little Rock crisis on CBS's "Face the Nation" and NBC's "Today Show." He was called a "nigger-lover" and a liberal by conservatives.)

30, 1918, he implored his friend E. L. MacHenry to prop him up with pillows in the back seat of his car so that pedestrians could not see that he was ill. He died the next day.

The Williams family was unmistakably stamped by Senator Clarke's political fortunes and the life that accompanied his rise. Francis' mother Marion ("Mimi") vividly remembers her girlhood in Washington, where she attended Wilson's Inaugural Ball, White House parties under Taft, and spent some years at the fashionable Briar Cliff School. It followed that "Mimi's" daughter and only child was born into a world patterned on a clear social design. She attended the Madeira School, then on to Vassar, and crowned her debut in 1936 with a tour through Europe. Not surprisingly, she found Tucker's isolation, cotton, sharecroppers, mules, and taskmaster nature a sharp contrast to the social exigencies that directed her family's lives.

Making Two Worlds One. The couple moved to New Mexico after the War, for Everett's health when Bobby was 2½ years old. Again in Little Rock after Tuck's recovery in 1948, they renewed their ties with Tucker. Everett III (Rett) and Marion were born in Little Rock after they returned. Though he worked in Little Rock during the week, Tuck never failed to spend his Saturdays on his plantation home. Everett, Sr. and his wife Will Lynne welcomed them to Arkansas, as did Tuck's maternal grandmother "Dan," who was then teaching at Tucker School.

The young Tuckers organized their holidays around the plantation. Christmas dinner was a Tucker event, and today its rituals co-mingle with the traditional Williams Christmas Eve. A Tucker plantation cook is the current "Turkey-fixer," and "Dan's" obligatory Christmas carols on the piano have survived through a musical daughter-in-law. On the Williams side, Grandmother "Mimi" still makes the cranberries and chocolate ice box cake. Long ago the young Tuckers added ice cream in holiday shapes to the meal, and they would be disappointed if their grown children didn't squabble over whether they received "Santies" or "Trees."

Meanwhile, life on the plantation was changing. Machines were becoming rivals to sturdy sharecropper arms and backs. Tuck, the planter's son, watched their cabins lapse gradually, then more quickly, into empty silence. Sons and daughters of the old hands moved away to Little Rock, California, or Detroit, and renters filled their place. To the land they brought irrigation, machines, and expertise, but unlike the sharecroppers, little of their lives. The old community was breaking up; the fiefdom had become big business.

At the same time Tuck was finding a new context for his inherited role. On Saturdays, when he commuted from Little Rock to oversee his affairs at Tucker, he was still the plantation "Captain." But during the week he directed the Industrial Development Company, a quasi-public agency whose purpose was to attract industry to the state. He viewed his

A photo display. (Top, left to right) Francis holding Cissy; Tuck holding Cissy with Tate at side (at a favorite summer "escape," Ludington, Michigan); Marion with husband Rick Glatter (a "Yankee" from New Jersey); "Barney" the Tucker family dog; (middle, left to right) Cissy Tucker (Cathryn Francis) with a duck hunter's cap; Rett holding daughter Cissy in front of Trinity Episcopal Cathedral; The Very Reverand Joel Pugh (Dean of Trinity Cathedral) holding Cissy; (bottom, left to right) Marion, Rick, "Mimi," Rett holding Cissy, Diane, Bobby, little Tate, Francis; Becky (Rett's wife) holding Cissy at cattle feed lot at Tucker; "Mimi" Williams and Santa with Cissy.

new job, not as a break with family tradition, but as a variation on an old theme. He explained: "As a descendant of the old planter aristocracy, I have had the interesting experience of feeling the need for industrialization. I used to think of it in terms of "Why can't we have a textile mill in Arkansas?" At that time cotton was shipped up to New England, and later the textile industry came down to the Carolinas and Georgia.

"In a few instances here in my time of industrial development, I have run across Negro descendants of people who lived on our plantation. They are now beneficiaries of whatever I had to do with bringing industry into the state."

But the question Tuck asks himself is how long the family pattern will survive. He takes heart in recalling: "When my father and I were the age of Rett [Everett III] and Bobby, we couldn't get away from Tucker fast enough." The bond came later, and because of it Tuck prefers to participate proportionately in the fruit of the land. His three renters pay him with crops, a fourth of the yield. Will he ever, like many Arkansas landowners, rent out his land for cash?

"It may come to that. It's frustrating because I've got the sentimental attachment. I was born and raised there, and I'm proud of it.

"I don't play golf, I don't hunt and fish and play tennis and what not. [The land is] sort of an avocation with me. I've got my little garden down there, and I can talk to my renters while I'm working in my garden."

He paused and reflected, then said sadly, "The next generation doesn't have that incentive." —Deirdre LaPin

PEDIGREE CHART

1
Robert W. "Bobby" 11.9.44
Everett III "Rett" 1.1.50
Marion Clarke "Baby Sis" 12.28.52
BORN
WHERE

2 Everett Tucker, Jr.
BORN July 7, 1912
WHERE Tucker, Arkansas
WHEN MARRIED Oct. 9, 1943
DIED
WHERE

3 Francis Marion Williams
BORN December 4, 1914
WHERE Little Rock, Arkansas
DIED
WHERE

4 Dewitt Everett Tucker
BORN March 11, 1880
WHERE Tucker, Arkansas
WHEN MARRIED Aug. 25, 1909
DIED May, 1958
WHERE Pine Bluff, AR

5 Will Lynn Alexander
BORN July 1, 1882
WHERE
WHEN MARRIED
DIED Oct 30, 1964
WHERE Pine Bluff, Arkansas

6 Robert Monroe Williams
BORN Feb. 25, 1891
WHERE Washington, Arkansas
WHEN MARRIED Feb. 28, 1913
DIED Jan. 12, 1958
WHERE Little Rock. Arkansas

7 Marion Clarke "Mimi"
BORN Jan. 18, 1893
WHERE Helena, Arkansas
DIED
WHERE

8 John Woodfin Tucker
BORN Feb. 22, 1845
WHERE Falkville, Ala.
WHEN MARRIED 1871
WHERE Tucker, Arkansas
DIED October, 1908

9 Sally Morrow
BORN May 11, 1853
WHERE Smyrna, Tennessee
DIED August, 1934
WHERE Tucker, Arkansas

10 Dr. Wm James Alexander
BORN 1848
WHERE Holly Springs, Arkansas
WHEN MARRIED Happy Hill Pltn.
DIED Dec. 1881

11 Louise Edmondson "Dan"
BORN June 24, 1860
WHERE Holly Grove Pltn. (Phillips Co.)
DIED July 9, 1951
WHERE Pine Bluff, Arkansas

12 Nal Williams
BORN March 3, 1864
WHERE Washington, Arkansas
WHEN MARRIED Jan. 22, 1890
DIED 1905
WHERE Little Rock

13 Snow Stuart
BORN Jan. 1, 1867
WHERE Washington, Arkansas
DIED December 28, 1950
WHERE Little Rock

14 James P. Clarke
BORN 19 August, 1854
WHERE Yazoo Co., Miss.
WHEN MARRIED Nov. 15, 1883
DIED 1 October, 1916
WHERE Little Rock, Arkansas

15 Sally Moore
BORN Jan 28, 1856
WHERE Moon Lake, Miss.
DIED July 22, 1923
WHERE Battle Creek, Mich.

16 Charles J. Tucker
1800-1856

17 Anna Obedience Drake
1806-1865

18

19

20

21

22

23

24 Abner Bryce Williams
1828-1896

25 Anne Caruth

26 Alfred Oden Stuart
1818-1883

27 Sarah Ware
1833-1878

28 Walter Clarke

29 Ellen White

30 Francis Marion Moore
1833-1859

31 Nannie Warren
1833-1915

William Tucker

Sally Hix
William Drak-
Mary Woodfin

How to Go Hog Hunting
Or How To Be Your Family Folklorist

Perhaps the descriptions in this book have inspired you to do some hog hunting on your own. If so, you are already on your way to becoming a family folklorist. "How do I begin?" you ask. That question, you will discover, is answered more easily than its opposite: "How do I end?" Stephanie Dixon declared when we finished our interviews, "If I had known how much work this was going to be, I would have done it anyway." It is pleasant work, and how much you do is your own decision.

The dynamics of folklore as the handing down of traditional material necessarily influence the way we hunt down its forms, trap its fleeting moments, or smoke out memories that have temporarily retreated underground. Our catch is seasonal if we wish to document the live intensity of holiday customs; it is occasional if we seek stories, games, or musical evenings as they occur in their natural contexts. Even if we attack our prey indirectly by asking questions such as, "What did you used to do at Christmas?" the answer will most likely unfold over time. Days after the topic is covered in a tape-recorded conversation, the addenda begin: "One thing I forgot to tell you about Great Aunt Edith's cornbread stuffing recipe is that a Yankee taught her how to make it." (There are some pieces of information it is better not to record.)

And so it goes. Conversations filter back to mother, son-in-law, great-grandmother, uncles ... and aunts ... and great-uncles ... and cousins... and spur their enthusiasm for your mutual past. One time, a student approached me with a desperate expression: "My grandmother

147

has called me to come over and go through *another* box of old photographs!" Not only did he have a look, but he copied them, labeled them, and in addition recorded several hours of stories grandmother recalled about their fading images. The process of collecting is as unending as the process of folklore itself. But let us return to the first question: Where to begin?

Setting Out. In our media-charged age, we sometimes equate folklore field research with tape recorders, cameras, video equipment, and other varieties of hardware. They are fine, documentary devices, and folklore has advanced remarkably with their introduction. Machines, however, are only as observant as the people who use them. Any folklore project begins and chiefly depends upon our built-in primary tools: sharp eyes, keen ears, a patient heart, and an open mind.

Observation, then, is the first phase of family folklore. How would you define the boundaries of your nuclear and extended families as family folk groups? Do they include non-relatives? Who in the group are important tradition-bearers? In what forms do they excel? At what times do they perform? Who are the members of their audience? Such questions are a helpful starting point, and as a member of the family, you will probably be able to answer them yourself.

As you ponder these questions, begin an initial inventory. Using the examples in this book as a stimulus, note the folklore forms handed down in your family. Your list probably will contain one or two dozen genres that will constitute the core of your eventual collection. A notebook, preferably with loose leaves, will become the repository for your material. Use dividers to separate the forms. (If you have many, you will probably wish to combine short ones — proverbs, sayings, expressions, and so on — or those for which you expect little notebook material — home movies, for example.) Whatever arrangement you choose depends on the relative strength of the traditional forms in your family and your habits in organizing information for later use.

Start through the notebook, heading pages with labels such as "sayings" or "Christmas" and then filling them with as much information as you recall. At this stage, a summary or title for "stories," "recipes," or "songs" will be a sufficient reminder to collect a complete version later. All folklore communications take place within a folk "event," yet some events, such as "Christmas at Grandma's" are repeated as a part of tradition. For these celebrations you need to record in your notebook; (1) the setting (2) the order of activities that regularly comprise the event: opening snacks and conversation; kitchen duties; the Christmas meal and menu; opening gifts; singing carols at the piano; playing games; storytelling, reminiscing; the evening turkey sandwich; farewell), and (3) the participants. In your notebook, you will be able to add a commentary about the meaning, value, origins, frequency, and success of the individual folk items you list. The attitudes and expectations that surround folklore is a vital part of every folk tradition.

By the time you have covered three or four genres in your notebook, you will have accumulated at least half a dozen questions for Mom, your son Eddie, or Great Aunt Emily. Don't be shy. Ask. Your questions about family tradition prime the pump for concentrated interviews later on. If discussions about family lore are a common topic among your relatives, your questions will flow into the conversation with ease. Sooner or later, however, the counter-query will come: "Why do you want to know THAT?" It is simple enough to explain that you have come to recognize that a record of valued traditions will be fuller if you document them now. Or that you wish to write an article or school paper about your family. You might believe traditions are a dimension of family life that children and grandchildren will wish to learn about. Whatever you say, be forthright and plain spoken. Recognize that not every relative will understand or appreciate your effort. Some will have perfectly rational, private reasons for not wishing to respond: "I don't WANT to talk about the past. The past was too HARD;" "You know, son, we were sold round about that time, and we've never said much about it since;" "If my cousin Margaret knew I had told you what our original name was, she'd never speak to me again;" "Well, Elmer shot and killed a man and had to leave the state, but you don't want to know about that." Often the reasons for such reticence are cloaked in mystery, and at times their roots are never bared. A possible explanation, however, is that your relative genuinely desires to spare you embarrassment because of your family role. My grandfather, who sold whiskey for a distillery during much of his life, judged his working career an inappropriate subject for young, female ears. Whatever wisdom he had gained about bourbon was, when he spoke with me, reduced to the terse remark, "Well, if it's a hundred proof, I'd say it's all right." Had my grandfather lived longer, I might have grown into the proper researcher's role, but since his death, I have been able to gather his whiskey tales second-hand from cronies and close relatives.

The memorabilia section of your notebook will raise other kinds of questions: "Who was the "RDM" whose initials grace the family silver?" "How did great-great-grandpa make that old table?" "Is Great Aunt Emma's diary still in her sister's bottom desk drawer?" If the answers to these and other questions reside with relatives far away, letters and telephone conversations will yield at least preliminary information. A letter containing clear questions with generous space between for written answers will elicit an orderly response. (Courtesy suggests you provide a self-addressed, stamped envelope.) There is no need to demand an immediate reply. A good correspondent will consult his papers, phone his brother, or check a journal before sending back an answer. When the letter arrives, file it away in your notebook for future reference.

Old papers also provide unexpected insights into the personalities

149

of family members. Jean Jones of Little Rock wrote about the "treasure trunk" that belonged to her father:

Last January my Dad died. The first thing we did after the company left was to go through his trunk.

Daddy had entered the US Army in 1918 shortly after World War I began. He had gone through boot training in Biloxi, Mississippi, then had gone by ship overseas to serve in France. In the trunk we found his "dog tags," Purple Heart, and some stainless flatware that he used in the field. We found his military pay book recorded when he was on bivouac in France. There were several yellowed military newspapers dated 1918-1919 and a well-preserved map printed in 1918 of the bicycle routes in Paris . . .

Old land deeds dating back to the 1930s of the farmland that Mom and Dad purchased from his parents were interesting. We found a newspaper article reporting the capture by my dad of a dangerous criminal who was wanted in several states when my dad worked as a deputy sheriff . . .

During this past year I have regretted not talking more with Mom and Dad about their early childhood and their marriage and for not asking Dad what was in the trunk . . . Had I examined those items in the trunk twenty years ago, I would have learned that underneath Dad's strong, unemotional, unsentimental, serious exterior was a warm, loving sensitive man. Although I have always loved and respected Dad, I might have liked him better had I known what he was really like.

In Hot Pursuit: Contexts for Recording, Natural and Induced. Because folklore transmission is a process integral to living, it would seem that a natural context would be ideal for capturing fleeting traditional moments. Sometimes an old homeplace will stir nostalgic memories. Take a walk around the farm or the old store or peruse hanging photographs in the den. You may well discover that times when Mom is preparing supper, Uncle Frank has come for Saturday-night bridge, or sister Sue's wedding is in full swing are too busy to make a quality mechanical recording possible. A tape-recorder placed in a room filled with bustling people is likely to yield little more than recorded chaos. Once your family catches on to the type of information you seek, you may be able to organize quasi-folkloric events: a family storytelling evening, a "family favorites" meal, or an old-time game of poker complete with the usual ribs and insults.

Your research will also profit from scheduled interviews. A specially arranged time for re-telling stories, reminiscing, or discussing an old scrapbook promotes better concentration and fewer opportunities for escape. Every member of your family has material for your notebook. For your first interview choose someone who is knowledgeable, makes you feel comfortable, and is likely to enjoy your tape-talks. Schedule these conversations at the convenience of the interviewee and in so far as possible in his or her favorite place at home. Your research could be combined with visits to a shut-in, a lonely sister-in-law, a cousin bereaved by his mother's recent death.

Genealogies may provide a focus for initial interviews. The pedigree charts in this book suggest several ways to plot out lines of descent. Others may be found in the genealogy manuals listed in the Bibliography at the end of this section. As our case studies show, families expend varying degrees of effort in tracing their blood relationships. Few, however, would not welcome learning more. The kinds of questions asked by genealogists profit a family folklorist because they open topics he can later pursue in his own way. Genealogy defines the family boundaries; it clarifies naming traditions; it reminds you of relatives whose memories may aid your research. Furthermore, basic genealogical data can be obtained from many of the folklore items listed in your notebook; histories, ancestor stories, and character sketches go hand-in-hand with discussions of kinship ties. They may furnish dates and places of birth, marriage, and death. Personal histories refer to school, military service, public offices held, honors, church and club affiliations, employment, occupations, travels. Here is important data for your notebook and your pedigree chart.

Genealogical research will guide you into other folkloric domains. In the family Bible, a standard source for important names and dates, you may find, stuffed between the leaves, recipes, home remedies, or letters. The family cemetery plot may offer clues to national origins, economic status, esthetic preferences and tastes.

A serious genealogist will cross-check data from home-grown sources in the public library, courthouse, historical society, church, place of business and schools. The Arkansas History Commission in Little Rock houses the following materials: post-1850 slave schedules and mortality records, post-1790 census records, military records, Arkansas newspapers, county tax records, and a variety of other resources including cemetery lists, diaries, manuscripts, account books, personal papers, and so on. The Little Rock Public Library has a genealogy room on the second floor in which a large collection of relevant publications are shelved. But, back to interviews.

An interview resembles an impromptu drama by engaging designated players (the interviewer, respondent, and onlookers) in a loosely-planned script (schedule of questions) in an event that needs direction to achieve the maximum result. Ultimately, your style of direction will depend on the way you choose to document the interview.

By now, tape-recorders have proved to be the most functional, convenient, and complete method of preserving a conversation. They are standard equipment for nearly anyone whose job or avocation depends upon sounds including the spoken word. But however regularly recording machines appear in modern life, Aunt Bess may find even the slimmest cassette mildly intimidating. And, indeed, you may, too. No matter how strange the machine may appear to you at first, confident and relaxed management will quash Aunt Bess's qualms.

Some aunts and uncles, despite your winning efforts, flatly refuse to speak into the machine at all. Concealed equipment is *never* an option. Notetaking is. Jot down a few reminders to yourself without making Aunt Bess feel ignored and afterward retreat into the nearest coffee shop or corner and fill in everything you recall. Carefully planned questions will organize your memory. In an un-recorded interview a written list of topics is almost essential before you start.

Tape-recorders permit greater improvisation in a natural conversational style. Make your questions open-ended; let the interviewee tell the story in her own way. Encourage her digressions unless they move away from folklore subjects altogether. Be an interested and supportive listener ("Oh, tell me that story again. I love it"); if the speaker is reticent at first, try sharing some of your own lore. Never challenge or argue. Your manner will unnerve your relative and possibly close a fruitful avenue for research.

Making Your Mark: More About Recording. As an interviewer, you play many roles: relative, questioner, supportive listener, and information analyst. Introduce a tape recorder or camera into the situation and you add the role of technician. What kind of equipment should you choose?

Many cassette machines are designed with a built-in, omni-directional microphone. This device is convenient and unobtrusive, but its results are often poor. "Omni-directional" means that the microphone records a broad range of sounds. A conversation in the corner may be spoiled by automobiles passing by a window across the room or by laughter and closing doors in the hallway outside. Most tape recorders come with an external microphone that is semi- or uni-directional. If you sit at right angles to your subject and point the microphone in his direction, your voice will be clearly audible without unwanted, interfering noise. Find a quiet spot, turn off radios, televisions, and — if weather permits — air conditioners and fans. These tapes may be your grandchildren's only opportunity to hear your grandmother's voice. A high-quality recording will later repay your effort.

A 60-minute or 90-minute tape is preferred to the 120-minute, which has a tendency to tangle or break. Purchase cassettes with screws in the upper corners; they allow you to open the case for necessary splicing or repairs. If you are recording in your own home and near an electrical outlet, use the electrical adaptor. Batteries are expensive and run down quickly when they fail. Some cassettes "stick." Run your tapes through the machine once on fast forward to prevent unwanted stoppage or slowing down. Most important, discover the capabilities of your microphone. Hold it at various distances and angles to test the recording quality. If your machine has a manual volume control, adjust it to the best setting. Never hold the microphone while you record. Use a microphone stand or book as a prop.

Test your machine before you begin. Make an opening announcement: "This recording was made with (interviewee) about (subject) on (date, time) at (place) and with (your name)." Play it back; if things are running smoothly, stop, set the record button, and begin the interview.

The visual dimension of family folklore is as valuable as sound. Cameras may capture the expression and movement of a family storyteller, Grandma churning butter, family meals and gatherings, important keepsakes, furniture, or portraits on the wall. Keep people in your pictures. It will be more interesting to see Grandma with her butter churn than a churn alone by the kitchen stove. Make a special album for your family folklore photographs. Store slides in projector trays, sturdy boxes, or transparent plastic loose-leaf sheets. Negatives, too, should be stored in transparent sheets or, at the very least, cut into strips of six frames each and tucked away in a business envelope that fits into a pocket taped to the inside back of your notebook cover.

Tying It All Down: Preservation and Retrieval. Photographs, tintypes, and daguerrotypes from past generations deserve an archives of their own. All the more so if they are cracked, faded, discolored or if their negatives were lost long ago. Old photographs may be preserved and enjoyed through reproduction. If you are a photography buff, you might set up a photocopy stand in your office or home and re-capture their images yourself using a fine-grain, high-contrast film. Some commercial photographers specialize in copying old prints, although their charges are often high. A central archives, such as "Special Collection" in the Library at UALR will copy, catalogue, and store old photographs and will supply copies inexpensively to contributors. A home archiving system includes: (1) labeling all photographs on the back in soft pen or very light pencil the names of persons shown, the date, setting, occasion, and (if possible) the name of the photographer and the type of camera he used; (2) making contact sheets from old and new negatives and filing them in your notebook; (3) filing corresponding negatives and marking them and the contact sheets with a film roll "number;" (4) for each roll, make an index of the information on the back of each picture (use the numbers 1-20 or 1-36 on the negatives). Now your archives catalogue is complete. Print the photographs, store them in an album, and give copies to the relatives who furnished the originals.

Tapes require cataloging and indexing as well. Number all tapes, noting on the cassette face the name of the interviewee, date, and subject. Transfer this information to a page in your notebook marked "Tape Catalogue."

An index to the contents of each tape will make it far easier for you to listen to stories or descriptions again. Index soon after the recording was made. In this manner, flaws in your tapes or equipment become readily apparent, as do points of information that need to be clarified or pursued. Using the digital counter on your machine as a reference point, list the highlights of your conversation. Here is a sample index page:

Dixon 4

Interviewees:	Stephanie Dixon
	Beadie Estelle Johnson (Stephanie's grandmother)
	Willa Stein Odom (daughter of above)
Present:	Paisley (Stephanie's baby daughter)
	Kim (Staphanie's baby sister)
Time:	February 29, 1981
Place:	Stephanie Dixon's residence, North Little Rock.
Motive:	Stephanie's suggestion
Machine:	Sony 110-A cassette, external mike
Quality:	Good; some interference from Paisley rattling car keys
000	Chitterling suppers. Mrs. Johnson ("Maw Maw") doesn't recall their exact origin. Willa Stein remembers that they began about twenty years ago while the family was living in La Grange. The tradition began spontaneously because everyone enjoyed the company and the meal.
044	The meal: chitterlings, salad, french fries, a vegetable, another meat (pork chops or steak), vegetable bean salad. Usually cooked twenty pounds of chitterlings, although Maw Maw remembers thirty pounds once. Most of the family loved chitterlings. WS: "We didn't care if we didn't have anything else." Everyone came to the dinners. Maw Maw's five children; grandchildren had 2, 3, 4 children apiece at that time.
070	A "regular dinner." Held in November at hog-killing time. An adult's table and a kid's table were set up in the dining room. Stephanie: "It was a big deal when you moved up to that table; somebody had to die or move."
114	Christmas Eve. Everyone would spend the night with Maw Maw and Santy Claus would come. Then adults would go out and carol. The "Santy Claus" took place at 3:00 A.M. Then a great breakfast at about 4:00.
145	Easter hunts every year at Maw Maw's. Prize: "golden egg" — a silver dollar.
184	Story: "The eggs that got lost in the quilt box and sewing machine drawer."
200	Quilts: Maw Maw and her mother and her mother-

* * *

Later, a word-for-word transcription of the stories and a summary of celebrations and craft techniques may be attached to the index. Transcribed material is good reading, but it emerges from long and patient labor. Be selective about what you choose to transcribe. Whatever your choice, always copy down *every word*. Include laughter, pauses, interruptions from the audience, and any significant facial expressions or gestures you recall.

Now it's your turn. Get a notebook and go hunt those hogs.

Selected Bibliography

Folklore Methodology and General Folklore Studies

Anon. *Caring for Photographs*. New York: Time-Life Books, 1975.

Adams, Ansel. "Copying Techniques with Artificial Light." *Artificial Light Photography*. New York: Morgan and Morgan, 1968.

Allen, Barbara, and Montell, William L. *From Memory to History: Using Oral Sources in Local Historical Research*. Nashville, Tenn.: American Association for State and Local History, 1981.

Banks, Ann. *First Person America*. New York: Knopf, 1980.

Baum, Willa K. *Oral History for the Local Historical Society*. Nashville: American Association for State and Local History, 1969.

————. "Oral History, the Library, and the Genealogical Researcher." *The Journal of Library History* 5 (1970), pp. 359-71.

Brown, Courtney. "Oral History and the Oral Tradition of Black America: The Kinte Foundation." *Oral History Review* (1973), pp. 26-28.

Brunvand, Jan Harold. *The Study of American Folklore: An Introduction*. New York: W. W. Norton and Co., 1978.

Collier, John, Jr. *Visual Anthropology: Photography as a Research Method*. New York: Holt, Rinehart, and Winston, 1967.

Cutting-Baker, Holly, et. al. *Family Folklore Interviewing Guide*. Washington, D.C.: Government Printing Office, 1978.

Doane, Gilbert. *Searching for Your Ancestors: The How and Why of Genealogy*. New York: Bantam Books, 1974.

Dorson, Richard. *Buying the Wind: Regional Folklore in the United States*. Chicago: University of Chicago Press, 1972.

————, ed. *Folklore and Traditional History*. The Hague: Mouton, 1973.

Draznin, Yaffa. *The Family Historian's Handbook*. New York: Jove Publications, 1978.

Dundes, Alan. *Mother Wit from the Laughing Barrel*. Englewood Cliffs, N.J.: Prentice-Hall, 1972.

Evans, Eli N. "How to Interview Your Grandparents." Pamphlet distributed by the Kin and Community Seminar, Washington, D.C.: Smithsonian Institution, n.d.

"Folklore and Fieldwork: A Layman's Introduction to Field Techniques." Washington: American Folklore Center Publication No. 3, 1979.

Goldstein, Kenneth. *A Guide for Fieldworkers in Folklore*. Hatboro: Folklore Associates, 1964.

Greenwood, Val D. *The Researcher's Guide to American Genealogy*. Baltimore: Genealogical Publishing Company, 1973.

Ives, Edward. *The Tape-Recorded Interview: A Manual for Field Workers in Folklore and Oral History*. Knoxville: University of Tennessee Press, 1980.

Kyvig, David E., and Myron A. Marty. "Your Family History: A Hand-book for Research and Writing." Arlington Heights, Illinois: AHM Publishing Corporation, 1978.

Stevenson, Noel C. "Search and Research, the Researcher's Handbook: A Guide to Official Records and Library Sources." Salt Lake City: 1959.

Tallman, Richard and Laurna. *Country Folks*. Batesville: Arkansas College Folklore Archive Publications, 1973.

Toelken, Barre. *The Dynamics of Folklore*. Boston: Houghton-Mifflin Co., 1979.

Vansina, Jan. *Oral Tradition: A Study in Historical Methodology*, trans. H. M. Wright. Chicago: Aldine, 1965.

Weitzman, David. *Underfoot: An Everyday Guide to Exploring the American Past*. New York, 1976.

Williams, Ethel W. *Know Your Ancestors: A Guide to Genealogical Research*. Rutland, Vt.: C. E. Tuttle, 1960.

Yoder, Don. "Folk Cultural Questionnaire #37: Grandparents in Traditional Culture." *Pennsylvania Folklife*, 23, No. 2 (Winter 1974-75), p. 49.

"Genealogy and Folk Culture," *Pennsylvania Folklife*, 15, No. 1 (Autumn 1965), pp. 24-29.

Bibliographies and Guides

American and English Genealogies in the Library of Congress, 2nd. ed. Washington: Library of Congress, 1919.

Blockson, Charles L., with Ron Frye. *Black Genealogy*. Englewood Cliffs, New Jersey: Prentice-Hall, Inc., 1977.

Catalogue of Genealogical and Historical Works. Washington: Library of the National Society, Daughters of the American Revolution, 1940.

Ferris, William R. *Mississippi Black Folklore: A Research Bibliography and Discography*. Hattiesburg: University and College Press of Mississippi, 1971.

Flanagan, Cathleen C. and John T. *American Folklore: A Bibliography*, 1950-1974. Meluchen, N.J.: Scarecrow Press, Inc., 1977.

Genealogical Research: Methods and Sources. 2 Vols. Washington: American Society of Genealogists, 1960, repr. 1971.

Guide to Genealogical Records in the National Archives. Washington: National Archives, 1969.

Miller, Elizabeth W. *The Negro in America: A Bibliography*. Cambridge, Mass.: Harvard University Press.

Puckett, Newbell Niles, and Heller, Murray. *Black Names in America: Origins and Usage*. Boston: G. K. Hall and Co., 1975. (Contains a discussion of unusual black names, the frequency of some Christian names, and attempts to trace some non-Western names to an African origin.)

Randolph, Vance. *Ozark Folklore: A Bibliography*. Bloomington: Indiana Folklore Institute Monograph Series, 1972.

Ross, Margaret. "Grass Roots." A regular column in the *Arkansas Gazette*. (Discusses genealogical research on Arkansas families.)

Szwed, John F., and Abrahams, Roger D. *Afro-American Folk Culture*, Part I: North America. Philadelphia: Institute for the Study of Human Issues, 1978.

Williams, Ethel L. *Biographical Directory of Negro Ministers*. Boston: G. K. Hall and Co., 1975.

Family Folklore

Agee, James. *Let Us Now Praise Famous Men: Three Tenant Families*. New York: Ballentine Books, 1960.

Ayoub, Millicent. "The Family Reunion," *Ethnology*, 5 (1966), pp. 413-433.

Baldwin, Karen L. "Down on Begger Run: Family Group and the Social Base of Folklore." Diss.: University of Pennsylvania, 1975.

Bertagnoli, Leslie. *Family Photographs*. Ed. Robert Benson. Urbana, Illinois: Red Herring, 1978.

Boatright, Mody. "The Family Saga as a Form of Folklore." In Boatright, Mody, et. al., *The Family Saga and Other Phases of American Folklore*. Urbana, Ill.: University of Illinois Press, 1958, pp. 1-19.

Boshears, Frances. "Granddaddy Roberts," *Midwest Folklore*, 3, No. 3 (1953), pp. 151-56.

Brandes, Stanley. "Family Misfortune Stories in American Folklore," *Journal of the Folklore Institute*, 12, No. 1 (1975), pp. 5-17.

Brunetti, Michael. "Italian Folklore." *New York Folklore Quarterly*, 29, No. 4 (1973), pp. 257-62.

Carbo, Terry. "Faith Healing Beliefs of a New Orleans Family." *Louisiana Folklore Miscellany*, 2, No. 4, pp. 91-100.

Chalfen, Richard. "Cinema Naivete: A Study of Home Moviemaking as Visual Communication." *Studies in the Anthropology of Visual Communication*, 2, No. 2 (1975), pp. 87-103.

Cook, Ann; Gittell, Marilyn; Mack, Herb. *What Was It Like?: When Your Grandparents Were Your Age*. New York: Pantheon Books, 1976.

Cooper, Wyatt. *Families: A Memoir and a Celebration*. New York: Harper and Row, 1975.

Cutting-Baker, et. al. *Family Folklore*, Washington, D.C.: Smithsonian Institution, 1976.

Dargan, Amanda. "Family Identity and the Social Use of Folklore." M. A. Thesis: Memorial University of Newfoundland.

Espy, Willard R. *Oysterville: Roads to Grandpa's Village*. New York: Clarkson N. Potter, Inc., 1977.

Gallagher, Dorothy. *Hannah's Daughters: Six Generations of an American Family: 1876-1976*. New York: T. Y. Crowell, 1976.

Garrett, Kim S. "Family Stories and Sayings." *Publications of the Texas Folklore Society*, 39 (1961), pp. 273-81.

Giusti, Rosanna M. "The Life Cycle Beliefs of a New Orleans Family of French-Italian Background." *Louisiana Folklore Miscellany*, 3, No. 4 (1953), pp. 268-72.

Haley, Alex. *Roots: The Saga of an American Family*. Garden City: Doubleday, 1976.

Halpert, Herbert. "Family Tales of a Kentuckian." *Hoosier Folklore Bulletin*, 1, No. 2 (1942), pp. 61-71.

Hardin, William Henry. "Grandpa Brown." *Publications of the Texas Folklore Society*, 29 (1959), pp. 58-68.

Hawkins, Beverly. "Folklore of a Black Family." *Journal of the Ohio Folklore Society*. 2. No. 1 (1973), pp. 2-19.

Knapp, Mary and Herbert. *One Potato, Two Potato: The Secret Education of American Children*. New York: W. W. Norton, 1976.

Kotkin, Amy. "The Photo Album as a Form of Folklore." *Exposure*, 16, No. 1 (1978), pp. 4-8.

Kotkin, Amy J., and Baker, Holly C. "Family Folklore." *Childhood Education*, 53, No. 3 (1977), pp. 137-42.

Labarbera, Michael. "An Ounce of Prevention, and Grandma Tries Them All." *New York Folklore Quarterly*, 20. No. 2, pp. 126-129.

Lasch, Christopher. "The Family and History." *The New York Review of Books*, 13, November 1975, pp. 33-38.

Lockmiller, Earl. "Tales My Grandfather Told Me." *Tennessee Folklore Society Bulletin*, 17, No. 2 (1951), pp. 42-43.

Montell, William L. *The Saga of Coe Ridge*. Knoxville: University of Tennessee Press, 1970.

Moody, Anne. *Coming of Age in Mississippi*. New York: Dell, 1968.

Morgan, Kathryn L. "Caddy Buffers: Legends of a Middle Class Negro Family in Philadelphia." *Keystone Folklore Quarterly*, 11, No. 2 (1966), pp. 67-88.

Mullen, Patrick B. "Folk Songs and Family Traditions." *Publications of the Texas Folklore Society*, 37 (1972), 49-63.

Ohrn, Karin Becker. "The Photoflow of Family Life: A Family's Photograph Collection." *In Saying Cheese: Studies in Folklore and Visual Communication*. Indiana University, The Folklore Institute: Folklore Forum Series #13, 1975.

Randolph, Vance. *Hot Springs and Hell and Other Folk Jests and Anecdotes from the Ozarks*. Philadelphia: Folklore Associates, 1965.

Rennick, Robert T. "The Inadvertent Changing of Non-English Names by Newcomers to America: A Brief Historical Survey and Popular Presentation of Cases." *New York Folklore Quarterly*, 26, No. 4 (1970), pp. 263-82.

Roberts, Mary Eliza. "Folklore in my Father's Life." *Midwest Folklore*, 3, No. 3 (1953), pp. 147-50.

Schneider, David M. *American Kinship: A Cultural Account.* Englewood Cliffs, N.J.: Prentice-Hall, 1968.

Sewell, Helen Hughes. "Folktales from a Georgia Family: An Annotated Field Collection." M. A. Thesis: Indiana University, 1963.

Shannon, Gertrude Sprouse. *Tales Thrice Told or Family Folklore.* Nashville: 1961.

Taube, Kristi. "Family Folklore With a German Flair." *Journal of the Ohio Folklore Society,* ns 3, No. 1 (1974), pp. 17-19.

Watts, Jim, and Davis, Allen F. *Generations: Your Family in Modern American History.* New York: Knopf, 1974.

Zeitlin, Steven Joel. Americans Imagine Their Ancestors: Family Stories in America's Folklore. Diss.: University of Pennsylvania, 1979.

Eastern Arkansas And The Mississippi River Delta

Allsopp, Frederick William. *Folklore of Romantic Arkansas.* New York: The Grollier Society, 1931.

Anon. "Arkansas Talk: Plain, Fancy, and Sometimes Downright Obflisticated." *Arkansas Times* (March, 1979).

Ashmore, Harry S. *Arkansas: A History.* New York: W. W. Norton and Company, 1977.

Blassingame, John W., ed. "Slave Testimony: Two Centuries of Letters, Speeches, Interviews, and Autobiographies." Baton Rouge, Louisiana: Louisiana State University Press, 1977. (An excellent collection ranging from 1736-1878.)

Botkin, Benjamin Albert, ed. *Lay My Burden Down: A Folk History of Slavery.* Chicago: University of Chicago Press, 1945.

_____, ed. *A Treasury of Mississippi River Folklore.* New York: Crown Publishers, 1955.

Carter, Albert Howard. "Some Folk Tales of the Big City." *Arkansas Folklore* 4 (August 15, 1953), pp. 4-6.

Courlander, Harold. *A Treasury of Afro-American Folklore.* New York: Crown Publishers.

DeArmond, Rebecca. *Old Times Not Forgotten: A History of Drew County.* Little Rock: Rose Publishing Co.

Dorson, Richard M. *Negro Tales from Calvin, Michigan and Pine Bluff, Arkansas.* Bloomington: Indiana University Publications Folklore Series, No. 12, 1958.

Durning, Dan. "Those Enterprising Georges: Early German Settlers in Little Rock." *Pulaski County Historical Review* (June, 1975), pp. 21-36.

Fountain, Sarah Mosley, ed. *Arkansas Voices: An Anthology of Arkansas Literature.* Little Rock: Rose Publishing Company, 1976.

Guida, Louis, et. al. "Arkansas Blues Today." Living Blues, No. 32 (May-June, 1977), pp. 15-30.

Guida, Louis, and Thomas, Lorenzo. *Crazier Than a White-Mouthed Mule: Student-Collected Folklore, History, and Tales*. Little Rock: Arkansas Arts Council, 1981.

Hamilton, Emelou M. *Little Rock Album of the 1890s: The Mary E. Parker Collection*. Little Rock: James W. Bell, 1981.

House, Boyce. "Arkansas Boyhood, Long Ago." *Arkansas Historical Quarterly*, 20 (Summer, 1961), pp. 172-181.

Masterson, James R. *Arkansas Folklore*. Little Rock: Rose Publishing Company, 1974.

Morson, Donald et. al. "Negro Remedies Collected in Eudora, Arkansas, 1974-75." *Mid-South Folklore*, 4, No. 1 (Spring, 1976), pp. 11-24; 4, No. 2, pp. 61-75.

Palmer, Robert. *Deep Blues*. New York: Viking Press, 1981.

Quarles, Benjamin. *The Negro in the Civil War*. New York: Russell and Russell. 1953, repr. 1968.

Rawick, George P. *The American Slave* 1941, repr. Westport, Conn.: Greenwood Press, 1972. (Culled from the Slave Narrative Collection of the Federal Writer's Project. Arkansas Narratives vols. 8-11).

Saxon, Lyle; Tallant, Robert; and Dreyer, Edward. *Gumbo Ya-Ya*: A Collection of Louisiana Folktales. Boston: Houghton-Mifflin, 1945.

Siebert, Wilbur H. *The Underground Railroad From Slavery to Freedom*. New York: Macmillan Co. 1898, repr. New York: Arno Pross and the *New York Times*, 1968.

Simmons, William J. *Men of Mark: Eminent, Progressive, and Rising*. George M. Rewall and Company, 1887, repr. Johnson Publishing Co., Inc., 1970.

Simond, Ada DeBlance. *Let's Pretend: Mae Dee and Her Family Join the Junteenth Celebration*. Austin, Texas: Sevenson Press, 1971. One of a series of books on seasonal and holiday customs of Black families.

Sutton, Leslie Parr. *Ozark Elders*. Little Rock: Winthrop Rockefeller Foundation, 1981.

Thompson, Robert, and Cornet, Joseph. "Four Moments of the Sun: Kongo Art in Two Worlds." Washington: National Gallery Exhibition Catalogue, 1981.

Vaughn, Freddie, and Reuter, Frank. "Negro Folk Remedies Collected in Southeast Arkansas, 1976." *Mid-South Folklore*, 4, No. 2 (Summer, 1976), pp. 61-74.

Vlatch, John. *The Afro-American Tradition in Decorative Arts*. Cleveland: Cleveland Museum of Art, 1978.

Waltz, Robert. "Settlement in Arkansas." Diss.: University of Texas at Austin, 1958.

Wolfe, Jonathan James. "Background to German Immigration." *Arkansas Historical Quarterly*, 25, pp. 151-182, 248-278, 354-385.

Yetman, Norman R. *Life Under the "Peculiar Institution"*: Selections from the *Slave Narrative Collection*. New York: Holt, Rinehart and Winston, 1970.

Journals
American Genealogist
Arkansas Family Historian
Arkansas Folklore
The Backtracker (Northwest Arkansas Genealogical Society)
Center for Southern Folklore Magazine. Published semi-annually at the Center for Southern Folklore, 1216 Peabody Avenue, P. O. Box 40105, Memphis, TN 38104.
Folklife Center News. Published quarterly by the American Folklife Center of the Library of Congress, Washington, D.C. 20504.
Daughters of the American Revolution Magazine
Daughters of the Confederacy Magazine
Journal of American Folklore
Mid-South Folklore
Midwest Folklore
National Genealogical Society Quarterly
Quarterly Bulletin: The Sons of the American Revolution
Ozark Mountaineer
Southern Folklore Quarterly

Films and Discs
"Harmonize: Folklore in the Lives of Five Families." A 21 min. film by Steve Zeitlin et. al. Distributed by the Center for Southern Folklore, 1216 Peabody Avenue, P. O. Box 40105, Memphis, TN 38104.
"Home Movie: An American Folk Art." A 25 min. film by Steve Zeitlin et. al. Distributed by the Center for Southern Folklore.
"Not Far From Here." 2 discs of family stories and songs from the Ozarks. William K. McNeil and George West. Russellville: Carroll County Historical Society. Distributed by Arkansas Traditions, 1018 S. Rock, Little Rock, AR 72202.
"They Tell It For the Truth." A film about Ozark storytellers. Kathy Nichol and John S. Altman. Pentacle Productions, Kansas City, MO. Distributed by Films, Inc.